Jacobean Appliqué

Book 2 – "ROMANTICA"

JACOBEAN APPLIQUÉ

Book 2 – "ROMANTICA"

Patricia B. Campbell & Mimi Ayars, Ph.D.

Photography by Richard Walker, Schenevus, NY

American Quilter's Society

P. O. Box 3290 • Paducah, KY 42002-3290

PAT dedicates this book to
Marty Bowne
My mentor and dear friend.
She put my name in lights!

MIMI dedicates this book to
Arzie, Janine, and Audrey Lynn
Mother, daughter, and granddaughter.
My inspiration!

Every effort has been made to ensure that the instructions in this
book are complete and accurate.

For questions about information in this book
and workshops contact:
PATRICIA B. CAMPBELL
9794 Forest Lane
Suite 900
Dallas, Texas 75243
FAX 214/994-0977

Library of Congress Cataloging-in-Publication Data

Campbell, Patricia.
    Jacobean Appliqué / Patricia Campbell and Mimi Ayars; photography by Richard Walker.
       p.cm.
    Contents: Bk. 1. "Exotica".
    ISBN 0-89145-859-X (v.1):$18.95
    1. Appliqué – Patterns. 2. Quilting – Patterns. 3. Decoration and ornament,
Jacobean. I. Ayars, Mimi. II. Title.
TT779.C361995   93-11934
746.9 '7–dc20   CIP

Additional copies of this book may be ordered from:

American Quilter's Society
P.O. Box 3290
Paducah, KY 42002-3290

@$18.95. Add $2.00 for postage & handling.

Printed by IMAGE GRAPHICS, INC., Paducah, Kentucky

CONTENTS

INTRODUCTION

JACOBEAN APPLIQUÉ ROOTS

Jacobean (pronounced "Jack´-u-bee´-un") derives from "Jacobus Britanniae Rex," the formal title of seventeenth century English King James I, who succeeded Queen Elizabeth I. A distinctive style of literature, entertainment, furniture, architecture, and embroidery emerged late in Queen Elizabeth's reign and continued for more than a hundred years.

Jacobean embroidery differs from other forms of needlework, not by the thread or the stitch, but by the design — usually floral or arboreal with deeply notched leaves, undulating vines, intertwined branches and stems, coiling tendrils, and imaginative flowers. Birds often appeared in the greenery and small animals on the mounds. The thread ranged in color from deep green to contrasting rose, purple, blue, and gold — calming, soothing, muted. Glorious shading gave dimension to the botanical flora and fauna. An air of fantasy and romance permeated the compositions.

Treasured family pieces of Jacobean embroidery emigrated to America in the baggage of the English colonists. The needlewomen in our country changed the name to "crewel" (spelled a number of different ways), which referred to the soft, slackly twisted worsted yarn.

Some fine examples of early Jacobean needlework can be seen at Williamsburg, Virginia; the Henry Ford Museum, Greenfield Village, Dearborn, Michigan; the Shelburne Museum, Vermont; and Winterthur, Delaware.

Patricia B. Campbell has adapted old Jacobean embroidery patterns to new Jacobean appliqué designs, retaining the spirit of the antique pieces. EXOTICA (Book I) was designed for the novice Jacobean appliquér with nine blocks and a border to make a 65" x 65" (165 cm x 165 cm) wall quilt. ROMANTICA (Book II) was designed as a challenge to Jacobean appliqué lovers with 12 blocks and a border to make a 65" x 80" (165 x 203 cm) wall quilt.

ROMANTICA's designs are based on classic botanical shapes which have been simplified for appliqué. They focus on fantasy rather than realism. They are charming and fun to stitch. The book's instructions are explicit and user-friendly, with options offered. A discussion of color and fabric selection is included, plus guidelines for entering contests and winning over judges at quilt shows.

BOOK'S PHILOSOPHY

It's suggested that you follow the book's instructions for a trial period. "Try my way," Pat says, "and if you don't like it, try someone else's method or improvise."

There is no "must," no "have to," no "only way." The right way is your way. A freedom from precision exists with appliqué, unlike piecework. Enjoy that freedom!

Pat and Mimi conducted a workshop with 20 students prior to publication of this book in order to test the patterns. Seven of the students completed their versions of ROMANTICA. You can see from the photos on pages 156 – 157 that no matter how many people use a specific design, their individual creativity puts a personal stamp on their work. You can expect yours to reflect your personality.

Pat is your tutor, sharing tricks and epiphanies ("ah-ha's"), guiding you step by step. Mimi explains these steps with simplicity and clarity. Her graphic illustrations and Richard Walker's stunning photographs are great helpers.

QUILTMAKERS AND ATHLETES

Quiltmakers and athletes are kindred spirits. "What's that?" you say. They are! Serious quiltmakers and serious athletes use the best equipment available. They seek topnotch coaches and training opportunities. They absorb new information about their chosen field and consult with mentors. They practice faithfully, going through warm up and cool down periods dutifully. They devise a game plan. They dedicate themselves to excellence in performance. They enjoy competition, if not with others, then against themselves. They revel in accolades, awards, adulation. Athletes and quiltmakers have certain personal characteristics in common, too – patience, tenacity, willingness to overexert themselves, team spirit, vision, endurance, goal orientation, love of the game.

This book will be your "play book." It doesn't contain secret codes but code words that can be shared with everyone: perfect point, needle turn, skinny leaf, elongating point, V, U, butting up, heart-flip, and walking-backwards.

Chapter titles are borrowed from the sports world: Chapter 1, EQUIPMENT; Chapter 2, GAME PLAN; Chapter 3, WARM UP; Chapter 4, PERFORMANCE; Chapter 5, COOL DOWN; and Chapter 6, COMPETITION.

Serious quiltmakers as well as serious athletes use the best equipment available.

They are also alert to new devices and the improved use of old devices.

CHAPTER I – EQUIPMENT

LIST OF MATERIALS

A discussion of the items follows this checklist.

Checklist:

___ 45" (114.5 cm) background and binding fabric   5¼ yds. (4.8 m)

___ 45" (114.5 cm) contrast binding fabric (optional)   ½ yd. (0.5 m)

___ 45" (114.5 cm) backing and sleeve fabric   5 yds. (4.6 m)

___ design fabrics   variety

___ master pattern material   15" x 9 yds. (8.25 m) interfacing, examining table paper, or freezer paper

___ batting   69" x 84" (175.5 cm x 213.5 cm)

___ appliqué thread   variety, machine embroidery type

___ quilting thread   background fabric color

___ template material   clear plastic

DISCUSSION OF MATERIALS

■ Background Fabric (BF)

Background fabric is abbreviated "BF" throughout the book.

Resist bargain fabric; buy the best material available that you can afford. A 20-hour investment on an appliqué block deserves high quality, evenly woven 100% cotton for the BF. Gutcheon's® "American Classic" was used in ROMANTICA. It is excellent quality, comes in many beautiful shades, and the dye doesn't change from one lot to the next. It ravels, like all well-woven fabric, because it's perfectly on grain. Ask the clerk in the quilt shop to cut, not tear, your purchase. Tearing bruises, stretches and weakens the threads so that extra fabric must be allowed for the waste.

Although the layout in Fig. 9 on page 25 shows use of 5 (4.6 m) yards, an extra ¼ yard (0.25 m) is shown in case you want to pre-wash the fabric and it shrinks or in case the fabric was cut an inch or two short at purchase time.

■ Binding Fabric

Choose one of the dominant colors in the top and use that fabric for a contrast binding or, if you prefer the binding to be the same as the BF, see the layout in Fig. 9, page 25.

■ *Sleeve Fabric*

There is enough backing fabric allowed for the sleeve.

■ *Design Fabric (DF)*

Design fabric is abbreviated "DF" throughout the book.

100% cotton is the easiest of all fabric compositions to needle turn. The seam allowance rolls under with practically no effort. However, try other fabrics if you like. You can find good colors in blends, but they are less easy to work with than cottons. Rayon comes in beautiful patterns and shades, but is contrary, rebellious, hard to handle. It ravels badly and is very difficult to needle turn. Silks are lovely, but tend to wrinkle and flatten after being stitched. Sometimes the stitches show. Wool is bulky, linen stiff, velvet heavy. But try any that interest you.

Sometimes it's hard to tell 100% cotton from a blend. When shopping, look at the label on the end of the bolt. When using pieces from your treasure chest or that of a friend, burn a small piece in an ashtray. If the ashes are of the "blow away" kind, it's 100% cotton; if a lump results, a synthetic is present.

Collect fabric you think you would like to use in ROMANTICA. Go through your personal stash, exchange pieces with friends, shop for fat quarters. When you're gathering, pay no attention to "goes with" because you don't know yet in what combination you'll use them. A fabric can change from the way it looks by itself and the way it appears when placed next to another fabric.

■ *Master Pattern Material*

A number of materials may be used for the master pattern. Choose inexpensive, lightweight, non-woven, non-fusible interfacing (which comes in a package 15" x 3 yards (38 cm x 2.75 m), the paper that covers the examining table at a physician's office, or freezer paper.

■ *Batting*

Batting thickness is a personal choice, but because a wall quilt is not for warmth but for show, it can be lightweight polyester or cotton. Hobbs cotton Heirloom (80% cotton, 20% poly) was used in the featured quilt ROMANTICA. For a classic look try Hobbs Thermore. If you prefer a higher loft, Hobbs Polydown works well. Although you are not concerned with warmth for a wall quilt, Hobbs wool batt needles very nicely. Try it.

■ *Appliqué Thread*

In Jacobean appliqué you want your stitches to be hidden so that the design, rather than the stitch, catches the eye. Machine embroidery thread is best because it's thinner than regular sewing thread and hides well. Either Mettler #60 and DMC #50 machine embroidery thread is recommended. Avoid polyester thread because it can cut through the fabric. Silk thread can be used on cotton, but is expensive.

■ *Quilting Thread*

Quilting thread the color of the BF keeps the quilting from competing with the appliqué design.

■ *Template Material*

Templates can be made from a number of materials. Clear plastic is ideal because it permits an advantageous placing on the DF; you can see exactly how the piece will look when cut out. A pattern duplicated on paper can be laminated and used as a template, but it's opaque.

LIST OF TOOLS

A discussion of the items follows this checklist.

Checklist:

____ Scissors, 2 pairs   Embroidery scissors for
                          fabric; craft scissors for templates

____ Needles   #10 or #12 Betweens

____ Thimble

____ Pins   Sashiko, sequin, quilting

____ Pin cushion

____ Light box (optional)
                          Commercial or improvised

____ Pencils   Silver, white, mechanical lead
                          Grease (optional)

____ Eraser

____ Pen   One that makes
                          a permanent black thin line

____ Circle template (optional)   Commercial

____ Sandpaper board   Commercial
                          or improvised

____ Emery board   Artificial nail type

____ Bias making gadget (optional)

____ Styrofoam panels (optional)

____ Rotary cutter and board (optional)

____ T-square or ruler

____ Sewing machine

____ Good lamp

____ Iron and ironing board

____ Comfortable chair

DISCUSSION OF TOOLS

■ *Scissors*

To maintain the sharpness of your fabric scissors, use them only on fabric, never on paper or plastic. Gingher 4" embroidery scissors are recommended for cutting out the design pieces. Gingher appliqué scissors are for machine appliqué and are too heavy.

Use fine craft scissors on plastic and paper. Fiskar 5" scissors are excellent and easily controlled when cutting small curvy templates. Kitchen scissors are heavy and fatigue the hand.

■ *Needles*

A small needle makes a small hole in the fabric; a large needle, a large hole. A long needle, called a "milliner's" (#7 Sharps) or "straw," wobbles, bends, and is hard to control. A gold needle is like a nail. A platinum needle sounds romantic, but those who have indulged in the luxury of one suggest they bend. "My grandmother always said 'a needle may break but it should never bend,'" volunteered a friend. Save your money for a ring instead.

The smaller the needle the better, because it's stronger and doesn't bend. Only ⅓ of its length is needed for turning, so why push more through the material? Although the eye is small, the thread is thin, so threading should not be a problem. If it is, a threader is available for fine needles. A bit of advice from a fellow quiltmaker: Fray Check™ on the tip of the thread makes for easier threading.

You already quilt with a little needle. Why make a new acquaintance when you have an old friend? Clover needles are excellent. Try a #12 Between faithfully for a week. If a #12 feels foreign, try a #10. Experiment until you find a size you like. Always stitch with what is comfortable for you — not with what you're told is the right needle. Consider having a number of needles in use, like in quilting, to stop and start less frequently.

■ *Thimble*

A thimble is protection against puncture wounds from the blunt end of the needle. Sore fingers delay stitching, maddening for an avid appliquér.

■ *Pins*

Sequin pins, sometimes called appliqué pins, are especially good for holding circles and other small pieces in place until stitching is well started. If there is a choice of length, choose ¾"(2 cm). Avoid those sold in craft shops; they're thick and blunt.

Sashiko pins, also sometimes called appliqué pins, are really silk pins with glass heads and are very thin and sharp. Use them to pin pieces to the master pattern. They make no holes in fabric but they do make holes in fingers. Use them with respect.

Use quilting pins to make perfect points and, of course, for quilting.

■ *Pin Cushion*

A household with children, animals, and spouses who have magnetic feet needs a pin monitor. In the early days when pins were hand-made and expensive, needlewomen had a creative way to keep track of every single one. A design was made in the pin cushion with the pins. When one was missing, the owner knew and looked for it. Consider following their example. Glass headed pins help because they are easy to find when dropped. A strong magnet or a flashlight kept handy for a pin search is helpful.

Old-time needlewomen claimed that a pin cushion stuffed with wool batting or hair would keep needles rust free; one made with sand or gravel would sharpen needles.

■ *Light Box*

A light box is required if you plan to mark the master pattern on a dark background. A commercial one is expensive, but you can improvise in the following ways: 1) put a lamp under a glass top table; 2) pull apart a leaf table and place a piece of glass or a plastic desk protector over the opening with a lamp underneath; 3) try a lamp in a waste basket covered with glass or plastic; 4) tape the BF block over the pattern to a window.

An alternative to tracing will be discussed in the section on pattern transfer to the BF on page 27.

■ Pencils

Silver and white pencils show up best on dark fabrics; darker pencil markings on light fabrics. A mechanical lead pencil keeps its point and lets you draw close to the template. Regular lead pencils dull easily and stitching time is lost trying to keep them sharp. Berol Prismacolor® is soft, doesn't keep a point, and breaks easily, but shows up well on darks; Berol Verithin® is hard but marks too lightly for most people to see. These pencils can be purchased at craft or art supply stores. Grease pencil marks on plastic will wash off, leaving a clear template, but they are hard to sharpen. A yellow wax pencil shows up well on dark cloth, but will melt if touched by a hot iron, leaving a yellow mark where you may not want one. Check with your quilt shop to see if a yellow water soluble pencil is available. Always test a product before using it on your project.

■ Eraser

Ideally, you won't have any marks to remove from the fabric. Various claims have been made for removal: a clean "rubber finger," a cotton ball, cotton batting (for white or silver pencil), cheap hair spray, Magiscrib, Marking-Pencil Removal, and a formula of 3 T. alcohol, 1 T. water, and 2 drops of Joy. Try every suggestion of this type on a sample before daring to apply it to your needlework.

Speaking of mark removal, don't forget the old but tried method for removing blood: chew a piece of white thread and when well wet with saliva, dab it on the spot. The thread absorbs the blood.

■ Pen

For tracing the patterns in this book onto the master pattern, use a permanent black thin line pen, such as a Sharpie®. Avold using either a grease pencil or a ball point pen; they smear. Use a Sharpie® pen on the plastic templates if a black edge is desired.

■ Sandpaper Board

A sandpaper board can be fancy or simple, purchased or homemade — an exceedingly useful tool. It keeps the fabric from slipping and distorting the design piece when templates are being traced. Make one by gluing a sheet of fine sandpaper to plywood, a clipboard, or the inside of a file folder. From the first time used, piecers as well as appliquérs marvel at this "helper."

■ Emery Board

An artificial nail emery board is better than the regular type and is used to file any little peaks that result when cutting out plastic templates, particularly circles.

■ Bias Making Gadgets

Although bias can be made as our grandmothers did, there are wonderful gadgets available to ease the job. With Fasturn, beautiful bias can be made in finished widths from ⅛" to ¾" (3 mm to 20 mm). This tool can be purchased singly or in packages of three or six different sizes. If you want to purchase only one, buy the ¼" (6 mm) size. Bias press bars are plastic or metal (Celtic) and come in sets of several sizes. Also an adapter for making bias is available for most sewing machines.

■ *Styrofoam Panels*

After the DF pieces have been cut and positioned on your BF block, you will want to look at the arrangement from a distance to check on color, balance, harmony, and contrast. Inexpensive Styrofoam panels (available from the lumber yard) covered with flannel and attached to the wall are an ideal way to accomplish this. Hanging your blocks on this wall will help you "read" your fabric combinations from across the room. If space is at a premium in your house, make a portable wall 4' x 4' (122 cm x 122 cm) and store it when not in use, perhaps in the garage.

■ *Light*

A good light is essential. If you can't see, you can't stitch well. A 72W halogen bulb gives non-glare lighting from a cool bulb.

■ *Other Tools*

The other items are in the tool box of most quiltmakers who all have favorite gadgets.

ILLUSTRATIONS

Each block is shown with a color photograph, a down-sized diagram, and a full-size master pattern in quadrants. The bottom and right border pieces are shown in sections with down-sized diagrams and full-size master patterns that are to be rotated — not reversed or mirrored, but rotated — to make the top and left border pieces. These, plus illustrations and detailed instructions, will help you make an heirloom quilt.

NOTES ON PATTERNS AND INSTRUCTIONS:

1. The illustrations in this book use solid lines to indicate sewing lines and broken lines to indicate cutting lines. (This is the opposite of sewing patterns.)

2. "Stitch" refers to hand work; "sew," to machine work.

Jacobean appliqué quilts
appeal to us as a response
to the emotion of delight.

Chapter II — Game Plan

Quiltmakers, like athletes, devise a game plan based on knowledge of their field, expertise of coaches, and interaction with fellow team players.

COLOR

Color anxiety plagues many a quiltmaker. Symptoms include: fabric selection jitters, slavish devotion to somebody else's pattern, avoid-a-decision syndrome, never-trust-my-own-judgment mentality, better-safe-than-sorry philosophy.

A lively discussion ensued at a recent bee meeting in response to a newcomer's question: "How do you choose the fabric for your quilt?"

"I just tell Judy at Calico Cupboard what color I want and she picks out the material."

"I follow the photos in the book."

"No problem. I love blue so I just buy shades of blue."

"I go with the coordinates of the fabric company."

"Trial and error."

"Whatever's in this year."

"My friends and I pool our ignorance." Giggles.

"Nina's got color sense, so I ask her." A chorus of "yeah's."

If you see yourself reflected in these comments, you're going to love making ROMANTICA because you'll have a new freedom you may never have experienced before. You'll break out of the "everything coordinated" mold. You'll use a wide array of colors and prints. You'll try new combinations. You'll no longer walk following a leader, but discover you have wings and can fly.

Although a color dictionary names 4,000 colors and it's said there may be 10 million distinguishable colors, the quiltmaker is limited by what's available in textile dyes, what colors are in fashion, and what the manufacturers have decided to produce in fabric. Even so, the possibilities are extensive.

Color is cultural. Look at African Kente cloth, beautiful and expensive. The use of such dominant colors as royal purple and Halloween orange together is not uncommon, yet in American-made cloth this combination is rare. White is worn in our country by brides; in China, by mourners. In Japan light green is for youth; dark green for the aged. In America today blue is for baby boys and pink for baby girls, yet 100 years ago it was the reverse. Many Native Americans express the four points of the compass with color names.

Color affects emotions. Blue and green used together calm; red and yellow, excite. Subdued colors like dark purple give a feeling of richness and elegance; bright colors like hot pink express liveliness and gaiety. Dark tones like midnight blue seem sad and moody; light tones like dusty pink, frivolous. Does gray make you sad? And yellow, happy? Red, white, and blue, proud?

Color has invaded our language. When Helen Keller was asked if she could see color, she smiled and said, "Sometimes I see red" and then she added, "sometimes I feel blue."

Color is personal. What is the dominant color in your fabric treasure chest? In your home? Do you like cherry red and chartreuse together? Lemonade yellow and flamingo pink? These combinations set some people's teeth on edge.

There are folks who do seem to have an eye for color, just as some have an ear for music. Harmony and discord are generally associated with music, but apply also to color. The composition, whether consisting of notes or colors, is pleasant or unpleasant, jarring or soothing.

No one at the bee mentioned the terms *hue, primary, secondary, analogous, complementary, value, tint, intensity,* or *tone.* One person did mention *shade.* There are at least three languages of color, one from the physics world, one from the field of psychology, and one from artists. Even when these groups use a common term, it may mean different things. For example, they all talk about *primary colors,* usually naming red, blue, and yellow, but physicists also include green as a primary color. There is a profusion of color names and a confusion of color terms. No wonder quiltmakers are puzzled. Of course, you don't have to speak the language of color to create a beautiful wall hanging, but let's talk about some of these intimidating terms so you'll no longer be afraid of them. We'll use the vocabulary of the artist. A little basic knowledge of color will help in your fabric selection.

You've heard of the color wheel (a circle) since your school days, but a six-pointed star, composed of two equilateral triangles and forming an inside hexagon may be easier for quiltmakers to visualize.

You've probably heard of *primary* and *secondary* colors ever since you were young. Let's designate the points of one triangle red, blue, and yellow (the *primary colors*). Fig. 1 (page 16). Primary colors do not involve any other color and all other colors can be derived from combinations of them.

You may also recall being taught that mixing two *primary* colors in equal proportion produces the *secondary* colors: red and blue result in purple; blue and yellow make green; and yellow and red make orange. Let's designate the points of the second triangle purple, green, and orange. Fig. 2. Now the points of the star are red, purple, blue, green, yellow, and orange. Fig. 3.

Mixing any two adjacent *hues* (colors) produces a new *hue*. If we mix a *primary* and a *secondary* color in equal proportion, the combination is expressed as a hyphenated word with the *primary* color expressed first. Therefore, the points of the hexagon are designated red-purple (magenta); blue-purple (plum); blue-green (turquoise); yellow-green, (lime); yellow-orange (apricot); and red-orange (flame). Fig. 4. If we alter the proportion of one color to the other, the resulting color will reflect that difference. Look at Native American jewelry. Some turquoises are bluish and some are greenish.

Now we have a color star. Fig. 5. Analogous colors are neighbors. For example, red-orange, orange, and yellow-orange reside next door to one another. Fig. 6. *Complementary* colors are diametrically opposed; for example, red and green or yellow-green and red-purple. Fig. 7.

Painters generally mix their pigments with a palette knife or brush, but Impressionists like Seurat (who was sometimes called a pointillist) painted small dots directly onto the canvas, one next to another, letting the viewer's eye mix the dots to achieve the effect he had in mind. If we

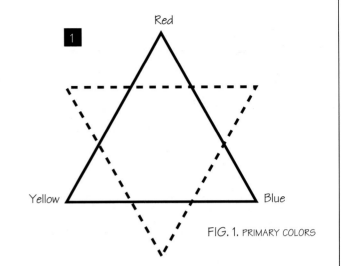

FIG. 1. PRIMARY COLORS

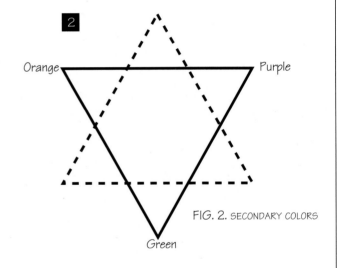

FIG. 2. SECONDARY COLORS

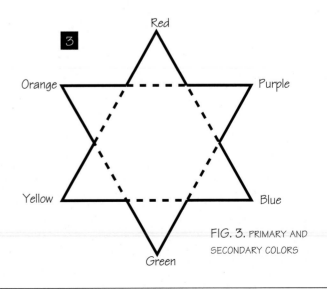

FIG. 3. PRIMARY AND SECONDARY COLORS

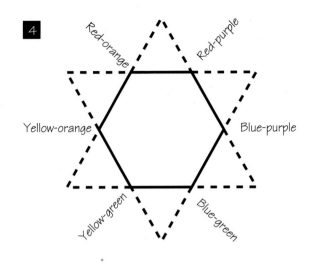

4

Red-orange Red-purple

Yellow-orange Blue-purple

Yellow-green Blue-green

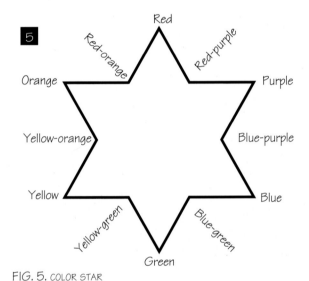

5

Red

Red-orange Red-purple

Orange Purple

Yellow-orange Blue-purple

Yellow Blue

Yellow-green Blue-green

Green

FIG. 5. COLOR STAR

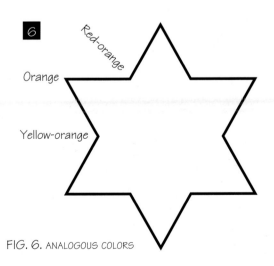

6

Red-orange

Orange

Yellow-orange

FIG. 6. ANALOGOUS COLORS

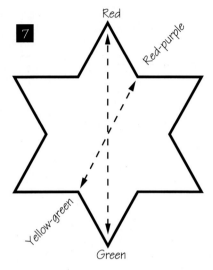

7

Red

Red-purple

Yellow-green

Green

FIG. 7. COMPLEMENTARY COLORS

stand close to a Seurat painting, we see only individual spots of paint; if we stand back, we see the composition. This is what happens with Jacobean appliqué; the colors merge in the eye and we need to stand back five or six feet to see the effect.

CONTRAST

Just as a realtor advises prospective buyers that there are three things to remember when buying property: "location, location, location," you are advised there are three important things in the making of a Jacobean appliqué quilt: "contrast, contrast, contrast." Contrasts in *hue, value, intensity, accent, temperature, tone, scale,* and *texture* as they apply to fabric, will be discussed later in the chapter.

Hue (Color)

Hues glow with contrast and are ho-hum without it. Compare the photograph of the two tulips (at bottom). The first is dull; the second, radiant. Contrast makes the difference. In one, the colors are closely related and boring; in the other they are "distant cousins" and entertaining.

One color can dominate, but the others need to enhance it. Reds and greens have been the most popular combination for quiltmakers down through the generations. You can't go wrong with letting these two colors predominate in your composition, but *complementary hues of equal amounts in the same piece of fabric should not be used because the eye in mixing them will perceive one hue – gray.*

Use any green with any other green; Mother Nature mixes them all together. A wide variety of greens is always needed, from the mysterious tone of a dense forest to the crystal *tint* of a shimmering iceberg.

Value (Light and Dark)

Value refers to the range of *tints* and *shades* of a specific color. When white is added to a pure color it lightens it. For example, white added to red results in pink (*tint*). The amount of white determines how light it is. Black added to a pure color darkens it. For example, black added to red results in cranberry (*shade*). The amount of black determines how dark.

The graduations from lightest to darkest are numerous. Fig. 8 portrays a small range of blues: baby blue, powder blue, sky blue are *tints* and cadet blue, denim blue, and navy blue are *shades*. Pure colors also differ in value; for

8

Key:

1-2-3   Tints
4   Pure color
5-6-7   Shades

1 – Lightest	Baby blue
2 – Lighter	Powder blue
3 – Light	Sky blue
4 – Pure color	Blue
5 – Dark	Cadet blue
6 – Darker	Denim blue
7 – Darkest	Navy blue

example, yellow is lighter in value than blue.

Although *tint* means pure color plus white, *pastel* is the popular term. Although *shade* means pure color plus black, quiltmakers commonly use *shade* to refer to all the *values* of a color from palest to darkest. Mint green, grass green, forest green we call *shades* of green. We say mint green is a light *shade* of green and forest green is a dark *shade* of green.

Two shades placed next to each other accentuate their difference, but when a number of different greens appear together, green, as such, becomes superior to any one of the individual green fabrics.

Intensity (High and Low)

Intensity refers to the degree of brilliance of a *hue*. The closer a hue is to the pure color, the higher the *intensity* and the brighter the hue is. For example, royal purple is of higher *intensity* than lavender.

Two contrasting colors with the same intensity used in equal amounts is like hard rock on a boom box. Two contrasting colors with the same intensity used in unequal amounts is like a polka on an accordion. Some colors are naturally more intense than others; for example, yellow is more intense than blue.

Hue, value, and *intensity* are interrelated. If you change one, you change the other two. For example, if you change the *hue* from pure blue to baby blue (now a new *hue*), you have changed the value (made it lighter) and the intensity (lowered it).

Accent

Accent is accomplished by using only a touch of a color, especially one high in intensity — like mustard yellow, hot pink, orange — in the same way that a chartreuse scarf gives zest to a Navy blue suit. The Amish know this fact well and use icy *tints* to spark their somber *shades*.

A fabric accent will do for your quilt top what a special spice will *do* for your recipe, but if you overuse a favorite accent color, then the purpose of scattered highlights is defeated. Some colors whimper, others scream. Keep the screamers confined to small areas.

Temperature (Warm and Cool)

Warm colors (reds, oranges, yellows) advance, excite, stimulate; *cool colors* (blues, purples, greens) retreat, calm, soothe. The warm colors pull and the cool colors push. Both are needed, each enhancing the other. One *shade* (or *tint*) of a color can be warmer or cooler than another *shade* (or *tint*) of the same color. For example, traffic-light red is warmer than barn door red. An illusion of depth can be created through the retreat of *cool* colors and the advance of *warm* ones.

Tone (Grayness)

Tone refers to the grayness of a color which results from mixing *complementary* (opposite) colors. Examples of complementary colors illustrated on our Color Star are red and green, yellow-green and red-purple. The resultant color is toned down or muted. Observe nature. Look at the grass. In the sun the color of the grass looks bright, vibrant (high *intensity*); in the shade, somber, muted, grayed (*toned* down).

Scale (Large and Small)

Printed fabrics with large patterns and printed fabrics with small patterns arouse interest. The large prints delight the eye and the small ones appeal to the emotions. The combination gives double sensual pleasure.

Texture (Rough and Smooth)

Texture usually refers to the tactile (the feel), for example, velvet versus silk. In Jacobean appliqué *texture* refers to the visual. One color playing against another creates depth, thus giving the appearance of texture.

HARMONY

Just as there is harmony in music there is harmony in color. You know how you feel when a singer hits a sour note. You get the same sensation from color disharmony. Color combinations pulsate, either like a toothache (bad) or like a heartbeat (good). They can be energizing interactions or enervating conflicts. Those color combinations that tend to vibrate can usually be harmonized by *toning* down one of them.

Analogous (neighboring) colors are always harmonious but often make a bland and uninteresting statement. A blue, blue-green, and green combination is pleasing, but lacks verve. Well separated hues tend to produce discord. Near relatives cooperate; distant ones, compete.

Too little harmony hurts our eyes; too much makes us yawn. Experimenting with your fabric stash will reveal which combinations are the most pleasing (*harmonious*) to you.

BALANCE (TRIANGLE RULE)

Although called a rule, the Triangle Rule is only a guide to check for color balance. If a specific color falls at the three points of a triangle, any size, any type (right triangle, equilateral triangle, isosceles triangle), in any position, there is balance. There can be any number of triangles.

The Triangle Rule helps you avoid the monotony of color distribution and also helps keep a specific piece from leaping out and punching you in the nose. If you want to check the color distribution in your quilt, choose one of the colors in your quilt and stick map pins into all the pieces that are that color. See where it is distributed. Try this with other colors, with each block and with the top as a whole. In checking for balance in your individual blocks and whole top, don't shackle yourself to this rule, but use it as a helper.

FABRIC SELECTION

How does this discussion relate to fabric? An appreciation of the basic color concepts gives you confidence in your fabric choices.

Background Fabric (BF)

Choose your BF first. Neutrals such as white, eggshell, ivory, chamois, tan, and gray are safe for background colors because a broad choice of fabrics can be used for the design pieces without conflicting with the BF. The character of the BF influences every DF piece that goes on it. No color exists in isolation. It's always interacting. There's always a relationship.

A tone-on-tone print is pretty and gives depth, but if it's a resist print, it's often difficult to appliqué and to quilt. Black – also a neutral – works wonders, especially if it's a velvety rich black.

Non-neutral background colors such as wine, navy, purple, pink, brown, and green are a challenge. Yellow, orange, and turquoise are especially hard to use as BF because they drastically limit DF choices.

Design Fabric (DF)

Although traditional Jacobean embroidery colors are soft and muted – green, indigo blue, brown, rose, and gold – bold and jewel-like colors are spectacular for Jacobean appliqué.

Don't worry about "goes with," for Jacobean quilts go with any decor. Strange as it may seem, since the patterns are based on antique designs, your ROMANTICA quilt can have a very contemporary look. With Jacobean appliqué you have the luxury of being able to use a wide palette of colors and a wide array of fabrics. Since ROMANTICA is pure fantasy, you can have purple leaves, if you wish.

Prints of two colors or two shades of one color give visual texture and a sense of depth, never achieved by solids. A black and brown combination print looks like the bark of a tree trunk. Multicolored prints are busy and distract. They cry out, "blend." In Jacobean appliqué you won't feel locked into blending colors. You're not buying a wardrobe or decorating a room.

Large multicolored tropical prints offer variety and a look of hand-dyed fabric. A small leaf can be cut from a large leaf, using the printed veins. Thus, you can have a three-dimensional effect without the use of embroidery.

Marbled fabric and batiks are overwhelming; use sparingly. Hand-dyed creations tantalize. Choose action-filled pieces with gradations from light to dark (several values). Light and dark contrast can create the illusion of illumination. Skydyes is the best for brilliant color, Country House Cottons for a sueded look, and American Beauty and Daffodil for the mottled look. Some hand-dyed fabrics are painted or have glitter added. If a piece feels stiff, it may be due to extra resin or salt in the painting process. If so, rinse in warm water. Of course, you can do your own dyeing, but don't underestimate the time and mess involved.

Solid fabrics can be used, but tend to appear flat. Use them in no more than 5% of a block; let the patterned fabrics predominate. If you really adore solids, go all the way with no prints at all. Were you to introduce a print, the viewer's eye would be drawn to it and it only. You want people to see the composition as a whole.

Pastels in Jacobean appliqué are not desir-able, but if you can't live without them, team them up with prints of medium value ("mediums"). Avoid lots of white in a print. It makes the piece itself look washed out or it fades away if the BF is light and it jumps out if the BF is dark. Geometrics are rarely useful, but plaids and stripes are exciting. Include them.

Contrast is the magic in planning a Jacobean appliqué quilt: different colors (hues), high and low brilliance (intensity), lights and darks (value), bright and muted (tone), cool and warm (temperature), large and small (scale), smooth and rough (texture), and accent. Having too little contrast is like not having enough salt in the soup. When contrasts occur, the result is variety, stimulation, depth, movement, drama.

To maintain color balance you'll want to use some fabrics throughout the quilt and introduce some new ones. Still others you'll sprinkle here and there for sparkle. High octane colors like lipstick red, chartreuse, watermelon pink, mustard yellow, pumpkin orange, electric blue, and dazzling purple give a quilt vitality. "Fire" or "lightning" in fabric calls out "look at me." Neighboring (analogous) colors are harmonious and go well together, but be cautious you don't overuse them and beget a blended top. Opposite (complementary) colors dazzle the eye when they are put side by side. Use them. Try any color and any combination of colors, but remember too much passion is fatiguing. Experiment — you can always discard something you don't like and replace it.

There are a few general guidelines in doing

these blocks. Each block can be thought of as a separate quilt. Consider not putting your boldest block in the center, for the center already catches the eye and you don't want it to get trapped there.

The usual greens and browns of vines and stems in nature lead to exhilarating reds, blues, pinks, purples, and yellows in the flowers. Your predominate fabric can be any color you fancy, but plan your flower elements so they will contrast to the stems and trunk. Don't be afraid to use fabric scraps for your flowers — old prints, new hand-dyes, or even fashion fabrics. Not enough variety is sleep-inducing; however, too much is nightmarish.

Don't stifle the impulse to try a combination. Go with the irresistible urge to experiment. Don't bank the fires of your temperament. Maintain your robust imagination in the use of fabric; remember Jacobean appliqué is pure fantasy. Never forget color is personal. Be adventuresome!

Most of us have some color sense and the rest of us can cultivate it. When you finish ROMANTICA you'll be well on your cultivated way. With experimenting and hands-on experience, you'll grow braver and your colors bolder. Your color awareness will also increase as you observe and analyze other people's work.

One difference between this game plan and an athlete's game plan is that for Jacobean appliquérs there are few rules. Suggestions and recommendations, yes, but few dont's. Options are offered and you choose. There may be easier ways or better ways, but there are no right ways. Your way is always the best way.

COLOR GLOSSARY

Analogous Colors — neighbors on the color star — e.g., blue and green

Complementary Colors — opposites on the color star — e.g., blue and orange

Hue — the name given to any color and used interchangeably with the word "color"

Intensity — brilliance of high or low degree

Primary Color — pure color, does not involve any other color — red, blue, yellow

Scale — the size of an area of color; e.g., in a print

Secondary Color — equal parts mixture of any two primaries — purple, green, orange

Shade — dark value of a color — e.g., burgundy (black with red) (Popularly used to refer to all the values of a color.)

Temperature — warmth or coolness of a color

Texture — visual impression of depth which gives three-dimensional effect

Tint — light value of a color — e.g., pink (white with red) (Often referred to as pastel.)

Tone — grayed values of a color, usually the result of mixing complements — e.g., red and green, blue-purple and yellow-orange

Value — lightness or darkness of a color

What we hear, we forget.

What we see, we remember.

What we do, we understand.

Chapter III — Warm Up

Quiltmakers as well as athletes undergo warm up exercises, not rushing to the performance unprepared.

To wash or not to wash is your call. Washing fabric before cutting is traditional and you don't have to worry about the fabric running or shrinking later, should you decide to wash the completed quilt. However, since ROMANTICA is a wall quilt, not a bed quilt, it is not likely to be heavily soiled. Dry cleaning preserves its brightness and maintains a crisp appearance and there's no risk of running. If you don't prewash, you can spend your washing time stitching. However, if you dry clean, choose a cleaner carefully. Ask if they have cleaned quilts before and what they do with them immediately after removing them from the solution. Ideally they will hang your treasure and call you. Pick it up as soon as possible and lay it on a bed until it can be re-hung.

CUTTING BLOCKS AND BORDERS

Press the BF before cutting. Cut twelve blocks 16" x 16" (40.5 cm x 40.5 cm) to finish 15" x 15" (38 cm x 38 cm), two borders 11" x 69" (28 cm x 175.5 cm) to finish 10" x 65" (25.5 cm x 165 cm), and two borders 11" x 84" (28 cm x 213.5 cm) to finish 10" x 80" (25.5 cm x 203 cm). Fig. 9.

A straight evenly woven fabric ravels. You can pink all the raw edges; zigzagging and serging distort. To insure that all pieces are on grain and exactly the same size, use a T-square or a ruler and the lines on your cutting pad. Follow Fig. 9 as a cutting guide and avoid the center fold of the fabric.

All the pieces must be cut from the yardage in the same direction. Mixing crosscut pieces with lengthwise-cut pieces and/or reversing pieces can cause a difference in appearance. The background should look the same all over the quilt top. To avoid rotating or reversing the pieces, tag each block as you cut it by stitching a small square of paper in the upper right-hand corner. Indicate "up" with an arrow. Fig. 10.

Tag each border piece as you did the blocks. Fig. 11. Notice that the top and bottom borders

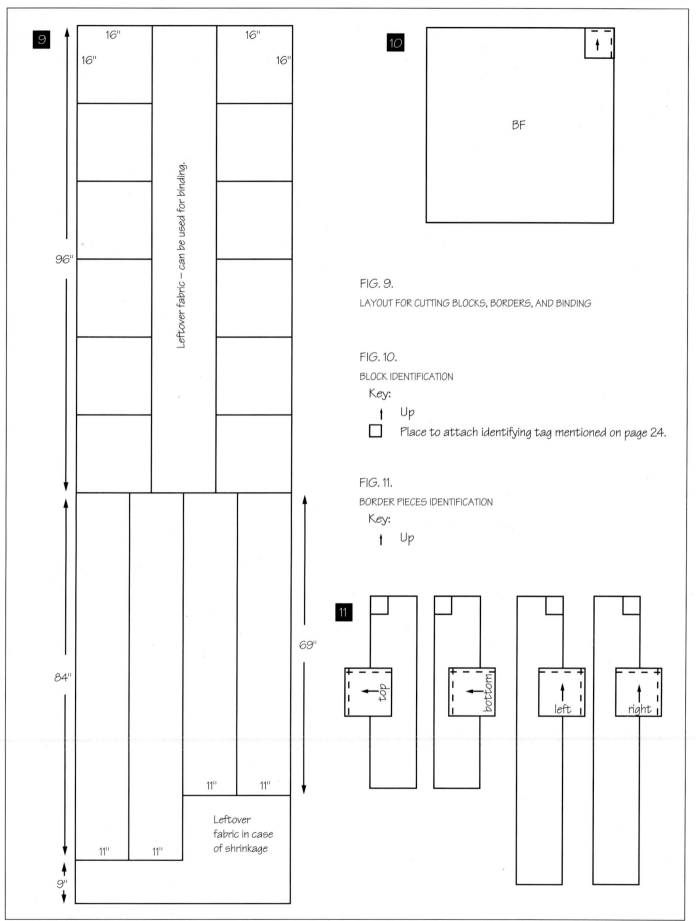

FIG. 9.

LAYOUT FOR CUTTING BLOCKS, BORDERS, AND BINDING

FIG. 10.

BLOCK IDENTIFICATION

Key:

↑   Up

☐   Place to attach identifying tag mentioned on page 24.

FIG. 11.

BORDER PIECES IDENTIFICATION

Key:

↑   Up

are tagged on the left rather than the right; also notice the direction of the arrows on those pieces.

MAKING MASTER PATTERN

You have the option of a number of materials for the master pattern: 1) interfacing (non-woven, non-fusible); 2) physician's examining table paper; or 3) freezer paper. Interfacing is inexpensive, portable, and handles like fabric. Physician's paper and freezer paper are translucent, pliable, and strong.

1. Cut 12 squares 15" x 15" (38 cm x 38 cm). Cut two rectangles 11" x 65" (28 cm x 165 cm) and two 11" x 80" (28 cm x 203 cm).

2. On one of the squares trace with a fine felt tip permanent black pen the quadrants of the full-size pattern for Block #1 (pages 60 – 63). Include on your master pattern the broken lines, the numbers identifying the templates, the letters showing the stitching order, and the arrows. You will notice that only Block #1 has letters and arrows. This will be explained later. Your master pattern should look like the down-sized version, only full-size (page 59). In one corner of the block write "#1," meaning "Block #1." Continue with the other blocks.

3. Trace the border sections in numerical order (pages 131 – 149). Include the broken lines, the numbers, and the "+" marks. You make only two master border patterns. In one corner identify the short rectangle as "bottom" and the long rectangle as "right." They will be rotated (not reversed or mirrored) for top and left. Your master patterns should look like the down-sized versions, only full-size.

MARKING PATTERN
ON BACKGROUND FABRIC

Find the center of the block by folding the square in half wrong side out, then in half in the other direction. Make a light pencil mark (on the wrong side) where the fold lines intersect. Fig. 12.

To trace the pattern on the background or not to trace is a decision you need to make at this point. If you're timid or new to Jacobean appliqué and wish to have guiding lines on your background, follow Option A, at least for Block #1. By the time you are ready to do Block #2, you may want to follow Option B. For those of you who hate pencil lines, follow Option B.

Option A — Marking

Tape the master pattern to a flat surface. Line up the center of the block and the center of the master pattern, then square the two. You can easily see through light colored fabric. Use a light box if you have a dark background.

We've been programmed for exact markings in needlework. If you *mark* exactly on the master pattern lines, you have to *stitch* exactly on those lines, which can be very frustrating. Marks must be covered when doing appliqué, which is not always easy, so make as few, as lightly, and as inconspicuously as possible. A single line can serve for a tree trunk, stem, vine, or swirl. Mark other lines on the BF ⅛" (3 mm) to ¼" (6 mm) inside the master pattern line to suggest where the pieces go. Put an "X" for the placement of the small pieces. Judges notice pencil marks and

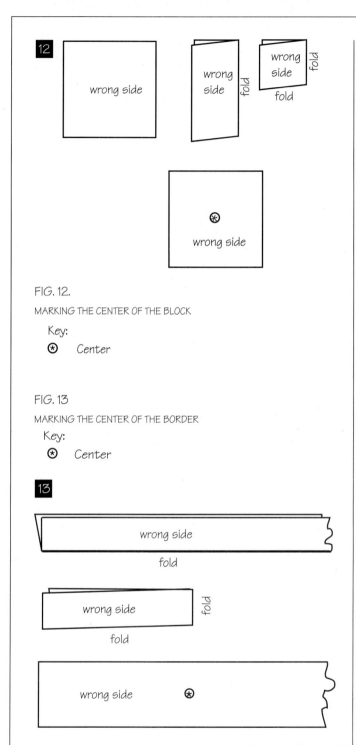

FIG. 12.

MARKING THE CENTER OF THE BLOCK

Key:

⊛ Center

FIG. 13

MARKING THE CENTER OF THE BORDER

Key:

⊛ Center

sometimes walk right by a fantastic quilt because of them.

Find the horizontal and vertical center of the background border pieces by folding each in half wrong side out, first one way and then the other. Fig. 13. Mark the center lightly with pencil. Line up the centers and square the short background rectangle with the short master pattern. Trace the pattern, being careful to stay inside the design lines as you did with the blocks. Repeat with the second short border (one master pattern, two borders). Continue with the long borders.

Do not mark on the BF any of the pieces with a "+" on them in Sections 1, 8, or 10 of the border pieces. These will be appliquéd after the top is assembled and you may wish to reposition them. Then you won't be handicapped by pencil marks in that area.

Option B — No Marking

An alternative to marking the design on the BF is to baste the master pattern (interfacing is ideal for this) onto the background block across the top, after matching centers and squaring the background and pattern. Then place a design piece under the master pattern in its appropriate place. Pin if needed. Lift the master pattern, flipping it over the top. Stitch that one piece in place. Neither hoop nor frame is used.

Appliquérs don't need to be captive to the color-within-the-lines mentality. If a piece is slightly off and there is a minimum of background markings, you won't have pencil marks to remove later. The no-marking method also gives you freedom from total concentration and the frustration of trying to achieve perfect placement.

MAKING TEMPLATES

Only a few template patterns – the tulip of Block #5 and the practice piece on page 150, and the border corner pieces on page 151 – are included. You'll make the other templates from your master patterns.

With a fine line permanent pen (if you want your lines to be permanent) or a grease pencil or a lead pencil (if you want to remove the marks and have a clean template), trace the templates on clear plastic. A permanent black line around the edge lets you see where the template ends when it's placed on the fabric, but some people find this a distraction. A clean template (you can wash off lead or grease pen-

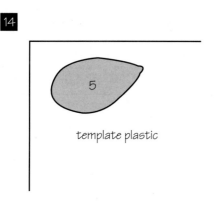

FIG. 14. TEMPLATE IDENTIFICATION
Key:
5   Template number
     for block

cil marks) ensures no accident of smudges on the fabric.

Identify each template with its piece number (1, 2, 3, 4, 5, etc.). Fig. 14. These numbers are for identification only and do not refer to the order of stitching. Pieces in a specific block or border that are the same shape have the same number, which means you need to make only one template for that piece, but as many design pieces as are needed. An example is the leaf numbered "15" in Block 1 that appears three times. You make only one template but cut three design pieces. Transparent plastic is ideal in letting you use the fabric to the best advantage because you can see the fabric underneath and choose the best area to cut the piece from.

Cut out the templates of Block #1. Store them in a plastic bag identified as Block #1. Pin the bag to the master pattern for that block. Cut out the templates for the rest of the blocks and the border, storing each group in an identified plastic bag and pinning each bag to the appropriate master pattern. Be sure to include the tulip template on page 150 in your Block 5 group. Cut out, identify, and store the corner template patterns together.

You want to stitch perfect circles. A perfect circle template is the first step. You can use a professional circle template purchased at an office supply store or you can trace the circles from the book pattern. When you cut out a circle template, make sure it is perfectly round. If it isn't, smooth the little jags with an emery board.

MARKING DESIGN PIECES

Separate your fabrics by color, type of print, etc. If two colors are dominant in one fabric, divide it in half and put a piece in each pile. Get well acquainted with your fabric; in fact, get intimate with it. Plan your block: tree trunk first, then flowers, and leaves last.

Start with Block #1. Lay the fabric right side up on your sandpaper board to keep it from slipping while you mark. Hold your pencil at an angle with the top tipped away from the template so that the pencil point angles into the template. This lets you mark close to the template and keeps the point sharp. These marks will disappear when you needle turn. Continue with the other pieces for that block.

> *Note:* Because you draw a solid line around the templates, the illustrations in this book use solid lines to indicate stitching lines and broken lines to indicate cutting lines. (This is the opposite of sewing patterns.)

There is an ongoing argument among appliqué teachers regarding cutting pieces on the straight or bias. Some judges insist that every appliquéd piece must be on the grain of the BF. Putting the design piece on its own straight is handicap enough, but having to put it on the straight of the BF is a double handicap. Bias is 1,000 times easier to needle turn than a piece on grain and there is minimal fraying and raveling.

Demonstrate to yourself whether you want your pieces on the straight or the bias. Cut a small oval. Locate the grain. Where will the most ravel be? On the straight! Every straight grain ravels. Where will the least ravel be? On the bias! Compare the areas of most and least ravel on each of the ovals in Fig. 15. Oval B will ravel less than oval A and will be much easier to needle turn.

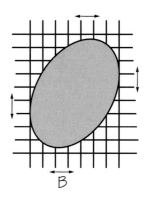

FIG. 15. AREAS OF MOST AND LEAST RAVEL
Key:
A   On straight
B   On bias
↕ ↔   Indicates area size of potential ravel

Grain going a number of different ways in your design pieces lends interest. Artists who paint short lines crossing one another haphazardly in every direction achieve texture. Similarly, the appliquér succeeds by using fabric bias. Cut as many pieces as possible on the bias. Don't hesitate to use a printed leaf for your leaf piece, cutting a small leaf to appliqué from a large printed one. Place a see-through template so that the printed veins become the veins of your leaf. Choose areas in a tropical print just the right shade for a lovely flower, regardless of grain.

CUTTING DESIGN PIECES

Cut the pieces out, adding a ⅛" (3 mm) seam allowance, yes, ⅛" (3 mm), not ¼" (6 mm). Less is better than more because the more allowance you have, the more you have to tuck under. A wide seam allowance creates a lump like dirt under a rug.

When cutting points, keep the tips pointed as in Fig. 16. There's no need to blunt cut the end.

On the inside of the tulip there is a straight edge and a scalloped edge. You'll notice that the space between these two edges allows for only one seam allowance, not two. Cut the fabric so that the allowance is on the scalloped side. Fig. 17. When you stitch, you will overlap the two petals of the tulip, hiding the raw edge. Cut a small rectangle for the area inside the "cup" of the tulip.

After cutting a DF piece, pin it in its proper place on the BF block. Following the composition check of your blocks, which you will do later, remove the pieces from the BF and pin them in place on your master pattern. This then becomes your portable "storage" block. If you plan not to mark on the BF, the master pattern will be basted to the top of your BF block so you will need to cut 12 squares and two borders of leftover interfacing or scrap muslin for your "storage" blocks. Pin the pieces in their approximate position on it.

Delay cutting the border corner pieces (marked with a "+") until everything else is appliquéd. Instruction on corners will be given later.

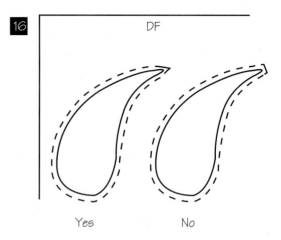

Yes   No

FIG. 16. MARKING AND CUTTING LINES FOR DESIGN FABRIC PIECES
Key:

Yes	Cut to point
No	Do not trim
- - -	Cutting line for 1/8" seam allowance
———	Marked template line

FIG. 17. CUTTING A TULIP
Key:

- - - -	Cutting line
———	Marked line

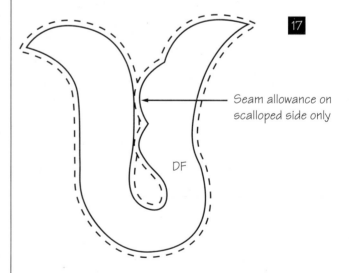

Seam allowance on scalloped side only

CUTTING BIAS

Blocks #1, #3, #4, #5, #7, #9, and #11 have bias stems. Choose the fabrics you would like to use for these. Every stem can be different or all the stems in one block can be the same or all the stems in the entire quilt can be the same. Be sure to press the material before cutting. Rotary cut minimum 1" (2.5 cm) widths; less width wiggles under the pressure foot on the machine. Block #1 requires 15" (38 cm); Block #3, 17" (42.5 cm); Block #4, 7" (17.5 cm); Block #5, 5" (12.5 cm); Block # 7, 3" (7.5 cm); Block #9, 2" (5 cm); and Block #11, 6" (15 cm).

You want perfect bias to make the stems, not only to be pretty, but to lie flat. If all the stems are to be made from the same fabric, you might use the continuous bias method, explained in many sewing books. However, you must cut absolutely accurately to get a perfect bias. Many people can't cut without getting slightly off; slightly off is bad news for appliqué. If it is not totally on the bias it will ripple, whereas true bias curves well. Cut away the bias seams that occur with this method. They're not pretty.

A square with pieces cut on the bias is more accurate than cutting continuous bias. A 9" (22.5 cm) square will yield 72" (180.5 cm) of 1" (2.5 cm) strips, more than enough for all the bias pieces in ROMANTICA. Lay the strips aside to be used later, having marked the right side.

CUTTING BINDING

The featured ROMANTICA photo shows a contrasting binding. If you like this look, pick out one of the dominant colors in your top and use that fabric for the binding. It makes an attractive frame. Cut 7 strips 1¼" x 44" (3.2 cm x 110 cm).

If you prefer to let the Jacobean border itself act as the frame, with the binding the same as the BF, there is sufficient fabric allowance, Fig. 9, page 25. Cut four strips 1¼" x 96" (3.2 cm x 240 cm).

Cut the ends of the strips at a perfect 45 degree angle so they are ready for sewing. Lay them aside for later, having tagged the right sides.

There is enough fabric allowance to make a double binding if you prefer the look of a thicker edge. With a wall quilt you don't need to be concerned about wear (which is usually the reason for a double binding). If you do fear wear, cut a second set of binding and put it with the leftover fabric to be saved until needed. ROMANTICA, as pictured, has a single binding.

You can use bias instead of straight strips, but you'll need additional material. A bias binding must be sewn on the quilt with great care to avoid stretching and making a wavy edge. Finger press the bias seams, rather than ironing them, for the same reason.

CHECKING COMPOSITION

As you cut each design piece, you placed it in its approximate position on a BF square. When all the pieces are placed, look at your block in terms of color, contrast, harmony, and balance. Squint your eyes. Look through a reducing glass or the reverse end of binoculars. Take a Polaroid picture. Let the block sit overnight and look at it again in the morning.

A Dallas artist suggests two tricks for checking on color and balance. Turn the block upside down and walk several feet away to view it. If the color and balance are correct, the block will be pleasing. If something is wrong, it will look like the flower is falling out of the picture. Hold a mirror in front of the block and look at its reflection. Because you are looking at the composition instead of the flower itself, a problem area will pop out.

You can also check for color balance by using the Triangle Rule on page 21. You want your top to sparkle, but not to startle. Don't let the eye become fixed on one spot. It should tour the entire top. Place the blocks in the area where you plan to hang ROMANTICA when it's finished because lighting is very important and affects the appearance of the colors. Does any one piece jump out or fade away? Does any part look like a hole? Don't be afraid to cut and reject. Anything you don't like, change, even the tree trunk which may not fit after the flowers and leaves have been added. Stitching will not improve the color.

When deciding if you want to use a specific DF, especially if you are replacing a flower piece, pull out an end of the fabric in a circle between your thumb and forefinger, making it look like a flower, and tuck it into another piece folded around it. You want it to look vibrant, not inert. When you're happy with the arrangement, carefully lay the pieces in their approximate place on the master pattern or your portable square and pin.

You can choose to cut the design pieces for all the blocks and borders at one time or to cut pieces for several blocks and look at them together, asking the above questions. Then cut several more. Repeat some fabrics; bring in some new ones. Watch for very bright blocks vs. very dull blocks. Check on contrast and color balance of each group and then again for the whole top.

An ideal aid to this process is a "wall" of inexpensive Styrofoam panels purchased from a lumber yard. Pin your work to the wall, stand back and "read" the fabrics from across the room. Using a reducing glass you can get a view of the whole. When you're happy with your placement of the design pieces, transfer them to your portable square.

If a group is making ROMANTICA, examine one another's blocks and borders. Point out what you like and make suggestions for those areas that bother you. That's what the participants in the pilot ROMANTICA workshop did. They fastened their blocks on the wall for critique and these are some of the comments:

"When I saw you were going to use that saffron colored background fabric, I thought you're gonna get into trouble, but you pulled it off."

"Those greens are like real!"

"Maybe Block 3 ought to be traded with Block 7. You've got two 'same color look' together."

"Block 6 is Dullsville; needs to be punched up."

"Look what that bright orange did? Wow!"

"The pale green background fabric looks pretty."

"Do you ever have an eye for color!"

"The printed veins on that leaf look embroidered."

"Where'd you get that gold? I need a piece of that."

"How many different fabrics have you got in that top?"

In this way you'll learn about color from one another. Expect to get braver and expect the colors to get brighter as you make more and more blocks. Improvise. Don't hesitate to replace a flower with a bird, add a butterfly, put a small animal at the base of the tree. Give ROMANTICA your stamp of individuality.

Appliqué is a rhapsody.

Jacobean appliqué makes my heart sing.

CHAPTER IV — PERFORMANCE

Quiltmakers like athletes are dedicated to excellence. They do what must be done to be the best they can be, to put on a first-class exhibition, and to take pride in their accomplishment.

GETTING READY

When you finish Block #1, you will have stitched convex and concave curves, "V's," "U's," perfect points, bias strips, and partial circles. Have the following items ready to start on Block #1: needle(s), pins, scissors, thimble, master pattern, BF block, DF pieces, and matching threads. Remember to match the thread to the design fabric, not the background fabric, and if you don't have the exact shade, go one shade darker, never lighter.

Create a stitching "nest" for many hours of pleasurable stitching. Seat yourself in a chair that fits. Put your feet up. This makes you lean back, not forward — a more relaxed position. Hold the stitching piece loosely in your lap, on a pillow, or with a lapboard under it. To maintain a comfortable position that will allow many hours of stitching time, the thumb of the hand holding the DF must face the thumb of the stitching hand. Fig. 18. Don't twist your holding hand; that will hunch up your shoulder, causing fatigue. Try a pillow under your holding arm. Periodically shake the tension out of your hands as if shaking off water. If you break for five minutes every hour, for an hour lunch, and an hour dinner, you can stitch late into the night.

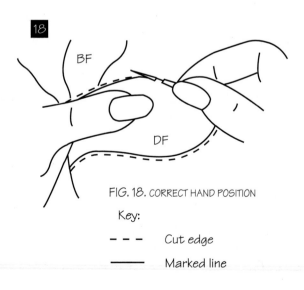

FIG. 18. CORRECT HAND POSITION

Key:

- - - Cut edge

——— Marked line

Place a good light over your shoulder on your left side, if right handed. (Right side, if left handed.) When you can't see, you can't stitch. Wear glasses if you have them. If you don't wear glasses but find yourself squinting or frowning, have your eyes examined.

As you stitch, you can listen to television, a VCR, books on tape, the radio, or talk to friends in person or on a speaker phone. You can daydream as you place a flower, leaf, or stem. Your thoughts can turn to world events or everyday chores, to reminiscences of your family. You can dream of the women who went before you or your present quiltmaking friends who share their tricks, often handed down from their mothers and grandmothers. Sometimes you will pay attention to how your fingers hold the needle or the fabric, what happens to the thread, how to manage a smooth round circle or a beautiful point. When you come to an obstacle, you can search your brain for something you read in one of your many books or learned from a workshop or a quilt celebrity. When you are relaxed, distress over some particular life problem lessens. Stitching should always be relaxing, a calming pastime. Think positive. Frustrations will then take care of themselves.

BASTING

Generally, you can baste the design pieces to the BF by placing a few pins here and there on the *underside* of the block, out of your way. This permits you to stitch without catching the thread. After the piece is partly stitched, the pins can be removed. You probably will want to thread baste tree trunks, because the shifting of such a large piece can be serious. Small pieces also shift sometimes. Don't fret about them. Just add an extra leaf or re-cut the piece bigger.

STITCHING

You may like to make a practice piece using the odd-shaped practice template pattern on page 150. Make a template, cut a piece of scrap DF, and a 10" (25.5 cm) scrap of BF, and appliqué. You will then have stitched a convex and a concave curve, a circle, a perfect point, a skinny leaf, a "V," and a "U."

Starting

The order in which you stitch the pieces does not matter except where pieces overlap. Overlaps are shown by arrows. You have copied these on your master pattern of Block #1. The shaft of the arrow is the "under" piece; the arrow point, the "over" piece. Fig. 19. The arrows act as reminders and let you move around the block, which is much more entertaining than stitching one area at a time. You might do all the "under" pieces for that

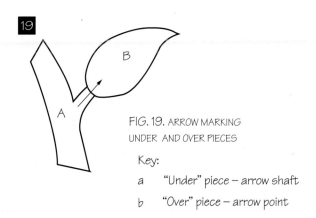

FIG. 19. ARROW MARKING UNDER AND OVER PIECES

Key:

a   "Under" piece – arrow shaft

b   "Over" piece – arrow point

block first, so you won't forget later. The part of a piece which is under another piece doesn't have to be stitched down. To help you get started, arrows are printed on the quadrants of the full-size pattern of Block #1 (pages 60 – 63). Consider marking arrows on all your master patterns.

Generally move only one piece at a time from your storage block to your BF square, except for the flowers. Move the whole flower unit and pin in place. Put pins on the back, remember.

Cut a thread (matching the DF piece, not the BF) 15" to 18" (38 cm to 46 cm) long. Longer will tangle or fray. Cut the thread on an angle, thread the needle (#10 or #12 Betweens), and knot, all on the same end – that which comes off the spool last. Use any knot you like: the one your mama taught you, the so-called quilter's knot, or your own creation. A workshop participant claims that running the needle and thread through a fabric softener dryer sheet keeps the thread from twisting.

The easiest place to start stitching is on a "straight-away" or on a gentle curve. Never start at a point. Using the tree trunk is a good starting place, but in Block #1 the piece identified as "5" must be stitched before the tree trunk because it's an "under" piece. Then do the tree trunk. Remember the numbers are for identification purpose only. They do not refer to the order of stitching. However, if you would like a suggested order of stitching for Block #1, follow the letters, A, B, C, D, E, etc. on the down-sized version (page 59). You can decide on the order for

the rest of the blocks and borders which do not show letters. After completing one block you will have a "feel" for the stitching order. Because tree trunks are usually the largest piece in the block, you may want to thread baste them.

Anchor your knot under the seam allowance of the DF so the knot will be hidden in the fold. Stitch counterclockwise. (Lefties, stitch clockwise.) This means the seam allowance is away from you, not toward you. Your thumb holding the piece is directly beneath your stitching. Fig. 20.

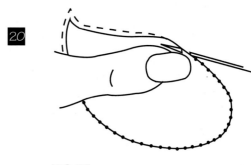

FIG. 20.
THUMB DIRECTLY BELOW STITCHING LINE
Key:

- - -   Cut edge

———   Marked line

• • •   Stitched area

A dark fabric will show through a pale one, which is unattractive. When that occurs, cut a piece of inexpensive voile, organza, or organdy the same size as your template, without adding a seam allowance. Sandwich it between the dark and the light. It acts like a slip under a dress or skirt.

Needle Turning

With the tip of your needle about ¾" (2 cm)

from where the thread comes up in the fold, sweep the needle toward you, turning the seam allowance under. Take several stitches and repeat. Always turn with your needle, never with your fingers. This technique eliminates pressing or basting. If the edge is not smooth, perhaps you are not sweeping under enough. A big sweep – ¾" to 1" (2 cm x 2.5 cm) keeps the edge smooth; a little sweep makes peaks.

The Stitch

Some appliqué emphasizes the stitching; Jacobean appliqué emphasizes the design and hides the stitching.

Directly out from where the needle emerges on the marked line and slightly under the fold of the DF, insert your needle point into the BF, pick up two or three threads and come up into the DF on the marked line (the fold) about ¹⁄₁₆" (1.5 mm) from the last stitch. The picking up of the threads and the emergence into the fold are one motion. Fig. 21. Don't fret if the stitches on the

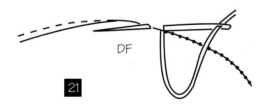

FIG. 21. NEEDLE POSITION FOR STITCH

Key:

– – –   Marked line and cut edge

———   Needle turned area

• • •   Stitched area

Area immediately left of needle has been needle turned.

back go in different directions; put your energy into having elegant stitches on the front.

Make your stitches perpendicular to the edge of the design piece. This will line up the stitches. The arrows in Fig. 22 show the angles of the stitches, not the distance from the fold. If you take a stitch too far out from the design piece into the BF, the thread will show. If you take it too deep into the DF, it will show. If your stitches slant, they will not only show, but also dimple the fabric. Stitches that are too tight fray the thread and ripple the design piece.

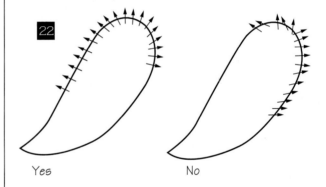

Yes   No

FIG. 22. DIRECTION OF STITCHES

If the stitches are not close enough, "eekers" will occur. Do you recall the cartoon of a woman on a chair with her hair standing straight out from her head, crying "eek," as she sees a mouse scurrying across the floor? Often when a thread from the fabric peeks out, the stitcher gasps, "eek!" Take your needle and push it back in.

There is no such thing as fray or ravel when you're stitching; consider it your seam allowance and tuck it under with your needle. There also is no such thing as ripping. It's "unstitching," as a child told her mother. Try not to "unstitch" because some threads stay in the BF, little fussy things that judges don't like.

Continue: needle turn, insert your needle barely under the DF into the BF, pick up two or three threads, come up into the fold from underneath, needle turn, pick up two or three threads, come up into the fold, needle turn. A rhythm and a constant tension on the thread, like in crochet or knitting, will produce stitches that are consistent and beautiful. To avoid discomfort in your wrists and shoulders, be sure your thumbs keep facing each other.

Follow the steps, imitating this method, for a few days. If you don't like it, go back to your old method or someone else's method. Do it the way you're most comfortable with and can get the best precision stitching.

To summarize the secret to hiding appliqué stitches:

• Thread that matches the DF piece exactly

• Coming up into the DF piece in the fold

• Going down into the BF a fraction under the fold and directly out in a straight line

• Pulling the stitch snug, but not so snug that it dimples the fabric

Stopping

When your thread grows too short to continue, put the needle through to the back of the BF, in from the edge of the design piece. Take a little "bite" of the fabric with the needle. Make a loop of the thread and hold it under your thumb as you

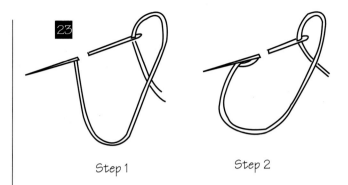

Step 1   Step 2

FIG. 23. FINISHING OFF KNOT

gently pull the stitch in place. Fig. 23, Step 1. Repeat, with a second "bite." Fig. 23, Step 2. Bury the tail by passing the needle between the two layers (BF and DF) away from the edge. Snip the tail close to the BF so there are no loose threads.

To continue stitching, cut a new piece of thread and knot it. Start with the needle point coming up at the marked line, very close to the last stitch. The new knot will be hidden in the fold. Proceed as before.

After the piece is appliquéd, end as you did when you ran out of thread. You don't want any loose threads showing through the BF.

CURVES

Convex

Convex curves (outside curves) are easy. Fig. 24. Choose a piece to appliqué that has a gentle convex curve. You don't need to clip the curve because the seam allowance is only ⅛" (3 mm), rather than ¼" (6 mm).

Concave

Concave curves (inside curves) are a little harder. Clip only when absolutely necessary,

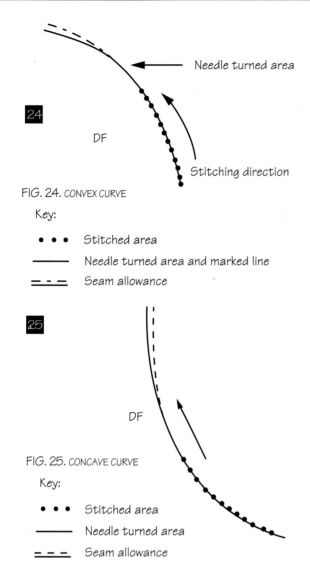

FIG. 24. CONVEX CURVE

Key:

• • •   Stitched area

————   Needle turned area and marked line

– – –   Seam allowance

FIG. 25. CONCAVE CURVE

Key:

• • •   Stitched area

————   Needle turned area

– – –   Seam allowance

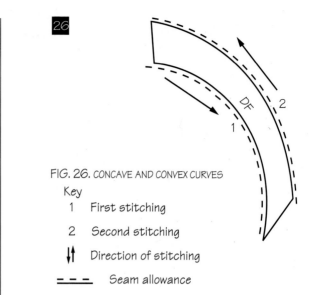

FIG. 26. CONCAVE AND CONVEX CURVES

Key:

1   First stitching

2   Second stitching

↕   Direction of stitching

– – –   Seam allowance

(inside) first and then the convex (outside). Fig. 26. If the outside is done first, the inside tends to pucker or gather.

"U"

You should have no problem with a "U," if you clip every ⅛" (3 mm) into the seam allowance of the valley before starting to stitch. Fig. 27.

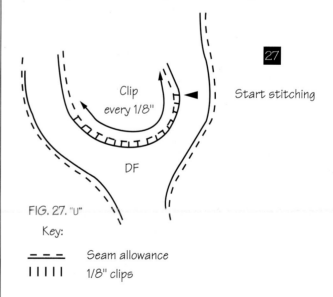

FIG. 27. "U"

Key:

– – –   Seam allowance

| | | | | 1/8" clips

which will be rarely because of the narrow seam allowance. Fig. 25. You'll know when you need to clip because you'll feel a drag on the needle or the seam fold won't stay folded. Listen to your fabric. It will talk to you: "clip me." When this happens, obey.

In one of the workshops a male participant groaned, "Oh, I'm in trouble now. My wife tells me I'm crazy to be a quilter. What's she gonna say when I tell her my fabric talks to me?"

When there are two curves — a convex and a concave one — as in a branch, stitch the concave

Perfect Points

This perfect points method will give you beautiful points. The instructions may sound complicated, but if you follow them step by step, you'll be delighted with the results.

1. Stitch, not to the end of the fabric, but to the marked point — the point where you start down the other side. Fig. 28, Step 1.

2. Take a second stitch on top of the last stitch (in the exact same spot) to secure that stitch, thus keeping it from moving.

3. Take your thimble off and set your threaded needle in the BF, out of the way.

4. Turn your block as if you were going to start stitching down the other side.

5. Clip off any little tail from the first side seam allowance that noses out. Fig. 28, Step 2.

6. Hold the thread and the stitch at the point under your thumbnail.

7. With a quilter's pin grasped about ½" (13 mm) up from the point and braced from behind with your middle finger to strengthen it (shorter is stronger), sweep the seam allowance under from right to left. Then sweep it back from left to right. (Left-handers sweep it left to right and then right to left.) Holding the point with your thumbnail, lift it only when you sweep the fabric under. If you don't like the result, pull the seam allowance out with your needle, and try again. To repeat: sweep the needle away from you, then sweep it toward you, carefully tucking under the seam allowance.

Sometimes the point frays and workshop participants panic. Don't let fraying intimidate you. Think of the remaining threads as the seam allowance. Just sweep them under and stitch. If you let yourself get frustrated, the situation will worsen.

8. Still holding the point tightly, turn the block so you can take a stitch into the BF about ¹⁄₁₆" (1.5 mm) out from the point. Fig. 28, Step 3. Unlike the other stitches, which you've been trying to hide, you now want this one to show. That extra stitch elongates the point. It will give the illusion that the tip is more pointed than it really is.

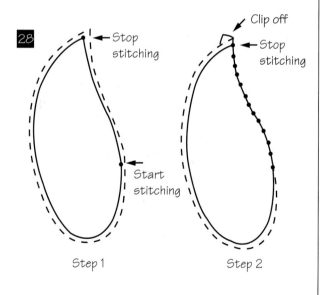

Step 1   Step 2

FIG. 28 STITCHING PERFECT POINTS
Key:

– – –   Seam allowance

• • • •   Stitched area

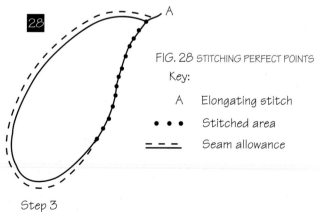

Step 3

FIG. 28 STITCHING PERFECT POINTS
Key:

A   Elongating stitch

• • •   Stitched area

– – –   Seam allowance

9. Proceed with stitching down the other side. When the appliquéd piece is finished, use your needle to shape the point and the heat of your thumb to press it.

After a week of using this point technique you'll be making sharp points without even thinking about it. The quilter's pin is the tool, but the real secret is the ⅛" (3 mm) seam allowance.

Skinny Leaves

Sometimes there are skinny leaves and sharp points at the end of slender tendrils. Even with these you can make perfect points.

1. Proceed as you did with perfect points, stitching to the marked end of the leaf.

2. Take another stitch on top of the last stitch to secure it.

3. Turn the stem back on itself and trim away any excess seam allowance near the point on the side you've just stitched. Also, clip away any loose threads and anything else that will be a hindrance or add bulk. This is fat removal: liposuction by scissors.

4. Hold your thumbnail on the last stitch with the thread under your thumb, out of the way of your stitching. With a quilt pin, sweep right to left and then left to right. (Lefties, sweep left to right and then right to left.)

5. Make an elongating stitch at the point.

6. Turn and start down the other side.

7. If it's still too wide, with your needle weave the thread back and forth across the point, catching only the seam allowance. Do not pull

too tightly because it will distort the shape.

A bump at the point? Too much fabric is turned under in the seam allowance. Beat it gently with scissors as tailors do. Now you know that "points with skinny tips are hard" is a myth.

Leaf Shading

As a spin-off of Nancy Pearson's "twisted ribbon" technique, here is a way to make a shaded three-dimensional leaf.

1. Choose a two-part leaf or cut a large leaf template lengthwise. Fig. 29, Step 1 (page 42). Use a different fabric for each part, light for one side and darker for the other.

2. Clip to the marked line across from each other on both inside pieces of the leaf. Fig. 29, Step 2 (page 42). Overlap dark and light parts alternately.

3. Using two needles and two shades of thread, stitch, making one section an "under," and the other section an "over." "1" is "under," "2" is "over" in Fig. 29.

4. Stitch the outside edge.

Block #3 has a leaf in the lower right corner that shows two short lines across what would be the vein line. Try this technique. Look for others that lend themselves to leaf shading.

Circles

Perfect circles result from being: 1) marked perfectly, 2) cut perfectly, and 3) stitched perfectly. No yo-yo's! No freezer paper needed! Use

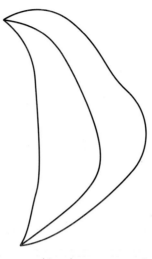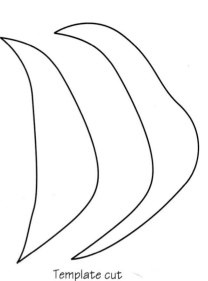

29

Step 1

Leaf template

Line drawn on template
where to cut

Template cut

FIG. 29. LEAF SHADING

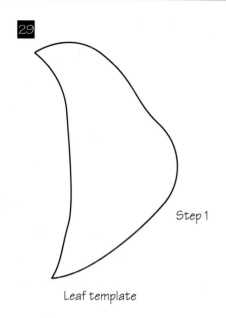

FIG. 29 DF PIECES CUT OUT AND CLIPPED

Key:
1   "Under" piece
2   "Over" piece
– – –   Seam allowance

a pin on the underside to hold the circle in place. Do not clip the seam allowance. Needle turn only enough to take one stitch. Turning under more will create points or a straight line. Take one stitch, turn the circle. Continue. Occasionally a circle ends looking like a spiral; that is, the last part of the circle does not meet exactly where you started. If this happens, snip the beginning knot, take out two or three stitches, reshape the circle, and finish stitching. One circle may take 10 minutes to do, but it will be beautiful. Treat ovals like circles. To repeat: needle turn for only one stitch, take that one stitch, turn.

"V"

Some valleys are deep and some, shallow (like between scallops). To make both types well-defined "V's" and not "U's," two different techniques are used: Heart-Flip for the deep "V's" and Walking-Backwards for the shallow ones.

Heart-Flip

1. Clip at the "V" to the marked line. If you clip too deeply into the fabric, don't worry. Just make the "V" a little deeper. Fig. 30, Step 1.

2. Stitch to the "V." Fig. 30, Step 2.

3. Fold under the loose side. Fig. 30, Step 3.

4. Take a stitch the same size as your others, not bigger, not smaller.

5. Press with your thumb.

6. Slowly bring the folded part back up.

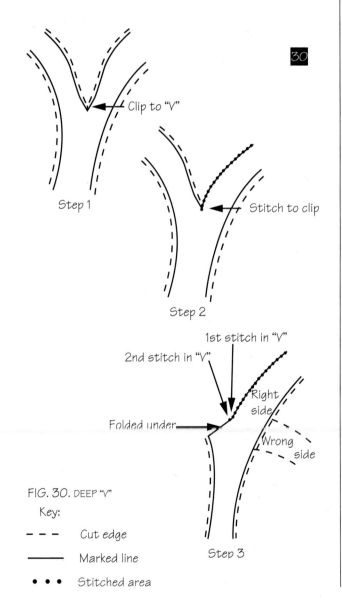

FIG. 30. DEEP "V"

Key:

- - - Cut edge

——— Marked line

• • • Stitched area

7. When you flip it back, the seam allowance on the flipped part turns under, ready for you to continue stitching. If stitches at the "V" show, it's okay, as long as they are no bigger than Lilliputian chicken feet.

Walking-Backwards

1. Clip at the "V." Fig. 31, Step 1 (page 44).

2. Stitch to the "V." Fig. 31, Step 2 (page 44).

3. Start needle turning 1½" to 2" (3.8 cm to 5 cm) away from the last stitch. Needle turn in tiny increments back down to the last stitch as if you were walking backwards, maintaining the curve. Take one stitch. Fig. 31, Step 3 (page 44).

4. Flip out the seam allowance that you've turned under with your needle. Fig. 31, Step 4 (page 44).

5. Proceed from the "V," needle turning enough for only one stitch. Take that stitch and needle turn for the next stitch. Repeat as with a circle.

6. Continue until you come to next shallow "V," when you will repeat the above steps.

When stitching a tree trunk or branch, stitch down one side and flip the rest down, using the Heart-Flip technique. If you have already stitched some part of the other side of the trunk or branch, then use the Walking-Backwards technique.

Tulip

Only one tulip appears in ROMANTICA (Block 5). A template is provided on page 150. Place it

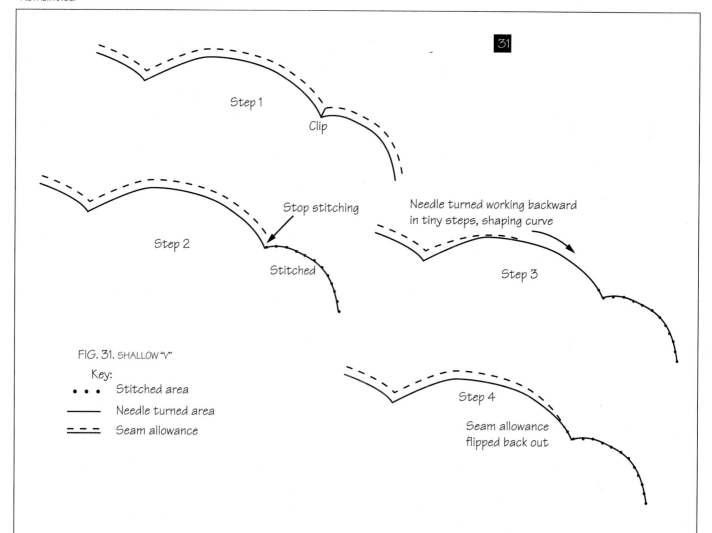

FIG. 31. SHALLOW "V"

Key:
- • • •   Stitched area
- ———   Needle turned area
- - - -   Seam allowance

on as much DF bias as possible. (Left-handers: flip the tulip template when placing it on the DF. Then the non-scalloped side will be on the right ready for you to stitch clockwise.) There is no hump at the fabric base of the tulip when you stitch, as you might expect, because the side is pivoted only slightly. This one piece will let you show off your skill in stitching a "U," a shallow "V," and two perfect points.

1. Clip the "U" at the inside bottom of the tulip every ⅛" (3 mm). Fig. 32.

2. Pin the side that has the straight inside edge. Put pins on the back, so they are out of the way.

3. Start stitching where indicated on Fig. 32.

4. Continue stitching around the straight side until you're opposite your first stitch.

5. Move the scalloped side over the stitched side just enough to cover the place where there is no seam allowance. Pin in place. Fig. 32.

6. Complete the stitching to where you started.

Butting Up

When two pieces touch each other without overlapping, it's called butting up. There is a natural tendency to start the second piece at the

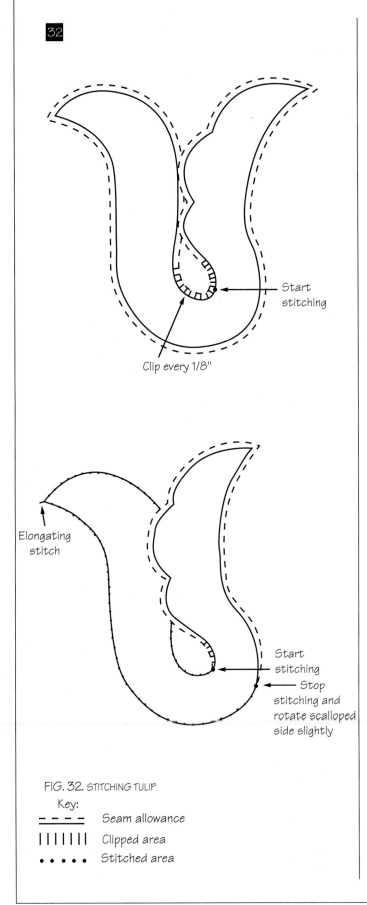

32

Start stitching

Clip every 1/8"

Elongating stitch

Start stitching

Stop stitching and rotate scalloped side slightly

FIG. 32. STITCHING TULIP

Key:

– – – – Seam allowance

| | | | | | Clipped area

• • • • • Stitched area

point of contact, but sometimes by the time that piece is completely stitched, the contact point either overlaps or falls short of meeting. If it overlaps, some can be cut off, but if it falls short of meeting there is trouble and you have to unstitch. The following will help keep them aligned. Fig. 33.

1. Stitch the first piece ("a") down completely.

2. Pin the second piece ("b") in place.

3. Start about 1" (2.5 cm) from where they are in contact, stitching toward the point of contact.

4. Make an elongating stitch to ensure that the pieces touch.

5. Continue stitching around the piece to where you started.

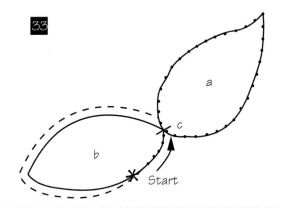

33

a

c

b

Start

FIG. 33. BUTTING UP

Key:

• • • Stitched area

– – – Seam allowance

a First stitched piece

b Second stitched piece

c Elongating stitch

Bias Stems

You have already cut the bias strips needed for stems in blocks #1, #3, #4, #5, #7, #9, and #11. There are a number of ways to appliqué bias. You choose from the following the way that feels right for you.

Option A — Grandmother's Way

Fold in thirds and baste. One raw edge is inside and the other is underneath when you stitch.

Option B — Bias Press Bar or Celtic Bar

Fold wrong sides together. Sew a bit wider than ¼" (6mm) from the fold. Make sure the seam is the same width throughout. Trim away the excess, cutting close to the sewing. Slide the ¼" (6 mm) bias press bar (Celtic bar) into the fabric tube just made. Move the seam to the underside and press. To avoid the need for repressing later, wrap the bias pieces around a paper towel tube.

Option C — Fasturn®

You can buy a single one or a set of six that range in size from ⅛" to ¾" (3 mm to 2 cm), standard or long length. Choose the ¼" (6 mm) size, if you buy only one.

Instead of sewing wrong sides together, sew right sides together with a seam a tad larger than the rod so that the tube will fit. Stitch across one end. Slip the metal tube cylinder into the fabric sleeve and then slip the curly pigtail into the cylinder. Twist gently until it grabs some threads in the end of the fabric. Slowly pull the pigtail and push the fabric. Voila! It turns itself inside out.

Option D — Center Baste

With the bias unfolded, baste the bias onto the BF where the stem is to be placed. In order to make sure the marked line is covered, the running stitch should be a fraction to the right of the middle of the bias but on the center of the stem design.

Trim away the extra fabric of the bias to the right of the running stitch and close to it. Fold the left side over and turn the raw edge under. Pin and stitch. This method is good if you want the bias narrow in one area and wide in another or if you have long stems. Don't choose this method for deep curves, e.g., a grapevine tendril, because it won't curve nicely.

Option E - Sewing Machine Adapter

Fold the fabric right sides together. Using the guide, choose the size desired. It keeps the stitch line perfect. If you sew a lot of bias, you need one of these wonderful gadgets.

Use the curve technique when appliquéing bias. Stitch the inside curve first and then the outside curve. It will lie perfectly flat. With the reverse, you'll discover little gathers on the inside that you won't like.

Roll leftover bias on a cardboard cylinder and save for future projects.

Appliquéing Border

After the blocks have been completed, appliqué the border. Be sure to stop near the corners where the pattern indicates. Make templates for the corner pieces (page 150) and cut out the DF pieces, but do not appliqué them until the top is assembled.

Chapter V— Cool Down

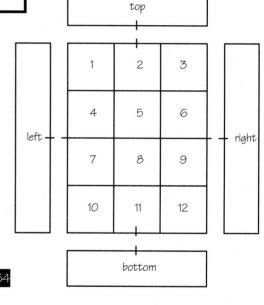

Quiltmakers like athletes go through a cool down period, taking care of unfinished details, cleaning up after the performance, tending to their own needs.

ASSEMBLING

Blocks

1. Lay the blocks out for assembling. You can follow Fig. 34 or arrange them to suit yourself.

2. Before you started to appliqué, you marked the center of the blocks on the wrong side. Fig. 12 (page 27). Measure out from the marked center in all four directions 7½" (19.3 cm). Fig. 35. With a T-square or ruler draw lines on all four sides for sewing. If you find you are short of the 7½" (19.3 cm), make it 7¼" (18.6 cm) or whatever measurement fits all your blocks. Remember you need at least ¼" (6 mm) all around for seaming.

An option is to make a 15" (38 cm) square of cardboard or plastic. Find the center by drawing diagonal lines. Fig. 36. Where the lines intersect, punch a small hole with the point of a compass

FIG. 34. LAYOUT FOR ASSEMBLING TOP

Key:

— Mid-points

top

	top		
left	1	2	3	right
	4	5	6	
	7	8	9	
	10	11	12	

bottom

34

FIG. 35. MARKING SEWING LINE FOR 15" FINISHED BLOCK

Key:

● Center

— Sewing line

- - - Cutting line

35

7 1/2"

7 1/2" ← ● → 7 1/2"

7 1/2"

or your scissors. If your block measurement is less than 15" (38 cm), adjust the cardboard template to comply with your measurement. Put

48

a pin through the hole and into the pencil mark on the back of your block. Square the template with the block, and draw around the four sides with a pencil. These will be your sewing lines.

 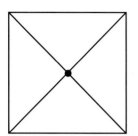

FIG. 36.
FINDING CENTER OF TEMPLATE SQUARE
Key:
● Center

3. Pin the top three blocks together and sew along the marked lines. Do the same for the next three. Continue for the other groups of three.

4. Trim away the excess fabric from the seams, leaving ¼" (6 mm).

5. Press to one side or open, as you prefer. Pressing seams open makes quilting easier.

6. Pin and sew the strips together, being careful that the blocks line up perfectly.

7. Trim the seams, leaving ¼" (6 mm). Press.

8. On the sewing line mark the center of each of the four sides.

Border

Fold a border strip lengthwise, right side to right side. Fig. 37, Step 1. On the wrong side mark with pencil 5" (12.5 cm) out from each side of the fold. Fig. 37, Step 2. Do this at intervals that can be connected by pencil lines drawn to indicate the sewing lines. Again, if you need to adjust your measurement to a smaller size, be sure you have enough for a ¼" (6 mm) seam allowance.

Pin, matching the center of the bottom row of sewn blocks and the vertical center of the bottom border. Be sure it is the inside edge of the border piece that you pin to the assembled blocks. Match the sewing lines of the blocks and the sewing lines of the border pieces. Sew, stopping ¼" (6 mm) from each end and backstitch. Trim the excess fabric along the seam but *not* the leftover fabric at the ends. Rotate and repeat for the top border. Continue with the right border. Rotate and repeat for the left border. Rotate; do not reverse or mirror.

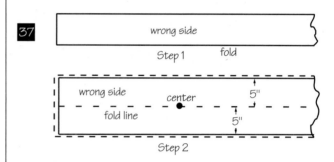

FIG. 37. MARKING SEWING LINE FOR 10" FINISHED BORDER

MITERING

Miter the corners using any method you like. An easy way to mark the 45 degree angle line is to use your cutting pad. Pin the miter lines and sew from the inner corner to the outer corner. Check for accuracy. Does it lie flat? If not, re-do. If so, trim the seam to ¼" (6 mm). Do this for all four corners. Press gently.

FINISHING APPLIQUÉ

You have made templates for those pieces marked with a "+." Trace and cut DF pieces for these. Position them where you like and appliqué. Trim the outside edges of the assembled top to

¼" (6 mm). Press the entire top on the wrong side with a dry iron.

CUTTING AND SEWING THE BACKING

1. Trim the selvage of the backing fabric.

2. Cut two pieces 84" (213.5 cm) long. Leave one full width 44" x 84" (112 cm x 213.5 cm) and from the other piece cut two lengths 13" (33 cm) wide, making two 13" x 84" (33 cm x 213.5 cm) strips. Fig. 38.

3. Cut a sleeve 9" x 65" (23 cm x 165 cm). There is enough fabric to make two sleeves, if you would like to have one also at the bottom of your wall quilt. Fig. 38.

4. Sew the three pieces together with ¼" (6 mm) seams, with the wide piece in the center. Fig. 39.

5. Press seams open or to one side, as you prefer.

BATTING

Cut the batt 69" x 84" (175.5 cm x 213.5 cm).

BASTING LAYERS

Lay the backing right side down on a table or floor, then the batt, and then the top, right side up. Pin baste or thread baste.

The backing is larger than the other layers. Fold the excess backing fabric to the front and baste to protect the edge of the quilt during quilting.

QUILTING

Quilting can be done in the open spaces and

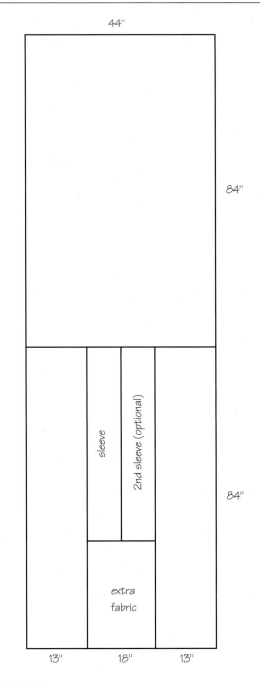

FIG. 38. LAYOUT FOR CUTTING BACKING AND SLEEVE

around the designs. Shadow quilt ⅛" (3 mm) and echo quilt three rows out from the design ¼" (6 mm) apart. Stippling or meandering quilting in the spaces where the blocks come together gives the whole top depth. Some of the flower and leaf templates can be used as quilting patterns. Hanging diamonds or crosshatch, especially dou-

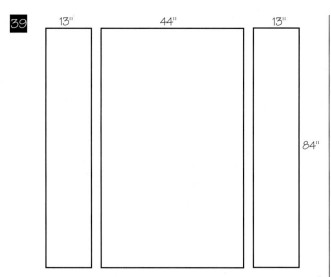

FIG. 39. LAYOUT FOR QUILT BACKING ASSEMBLY

bles, also work well. Use quilting thread the color of your background, so your quilting design doesn't compete with the appliqué design.

When the quilting is completed, sew with a basting stitch ⅛" (3 mm) in from the outside edge of the top all the way around. Trim the excess batting and backing even with the quilt top.

SLEEVE

1. Make double ¼" (6 mm) hems along each short end, turning ¼" (6 mm) under twice. Fig. 40, Step 1.

2. Measure 1½" (3.8 cm) from one of the long open edges. Fold along this line. Sew a ¼" (1.3 cm) seam with the basting stitch on your machine. Fig. 40, Step 2.

3. Fold the strip in half lengthwise with the open edges even (tuck on the outside). Fig. 40, Step 3.

4. Pin and sew the raw edges of the strip to the top of the quilt with a ⅛" (3 mm) seam. Notice it doesn't quite extend to each end. This

is to permit you room to sew on the binding and have the sleeve not show.

5. Pin and hand stitch the lower edge of the sleeve to the backing, using small stitches because there is tension on the sleeve.

6. After you've sewn on the binding, remove the tuck basting stitches. The tuck provides easement for the rod so that the quilt doesn't curl and the sleeve doesn't show across the top.

A second sleeve can be attached to the bottom. An inserted dowel helps the quilt to hang well. You can, instead, sew washers, drapery squares, or fishing weights into each lower corner, making sure they are well hidden.

BINDING

You have cut strips for the binding. Sew the strips together. Gently finger press the seams. Ironing may cause stretching, which may, in turn, cause the binding to wave.

Sew the binding to the quilt top as follows.

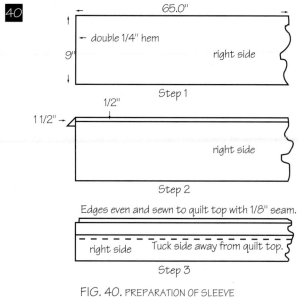

FIG. 40. PREPARATION OF SLEEVE

1. Lay the binding, right side to right side, on the quilt top, keeping the edges even. Start sewing about 6" (15 cm) from a corner, leaving a 2" (5 cm) tail unsewn. Fig. 41, Step 1. Sew carefully, maintaining an even ¼" (6 mm) seam.

2. Stop sewing ¼" (6 mm) from the corner. Backstitch and clip the thread. Fig. 41, Step 2.

3. Turn the quilt to the next edge.

4. Fold the binding on the diagonal (Fig. 41, Step 3) and then fold it back even with the top and side edges (Fig. 41, Step 4).

5. Starting at the upper edge, sew a ¼" (6 mm) seam allowance to within ¼" (6 mm) of the next corner. Fig. 41, Step 4.

6. Repeat the above instructions at each corner.

7. About 2" (5 cm) from the end, stop sewing. Cut off the remaining binding, leaving a tail of 3" (7.5 cm). Fig. 41, Step 5.

8. Fold the bottom piece "a" back diagonally. Fig. 41, Step 6.

9. Hold and sew the end piece "b" to meet the first sewing. Fig. 41, Step 7.

10. Trim the excess fabric.

11. Turn the binding to the wrong side, fold under ¼" (6 mm), pin, and stitch, using your newly-learned hidden appliqué technique. The stitches can be ¼" (6 mm) apart rather than the ¹⁄₁₆" (1.5 mm) you used on the design pieces. When you come to the corner, tack the miters down well, front and back. Be sure the corners are square. Push the needle back to the stitching line and continue stitching. At the point where the binding joins, trim the

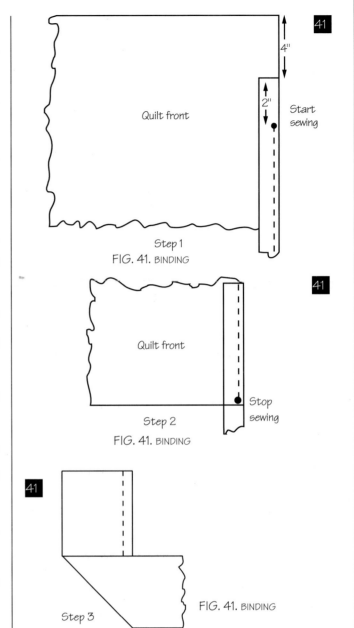

Step 1
FIG. 41. BINDING

Step 2
FIG. 41. BINDING

Step 3
FIG. 41. BINDING

excess, and stitch the front and back with your hidden stitch in such a way that it's hard to tell where you started and where you stopped. Don't press the binding; it tends to cause stretching. Quilt one row around the quilt on the inside of the binding.

DOCUMENTING

Future generations deserve to know about your quilt.

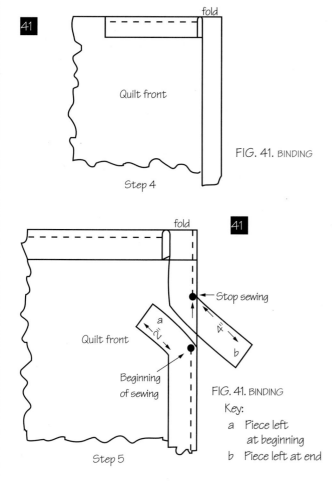

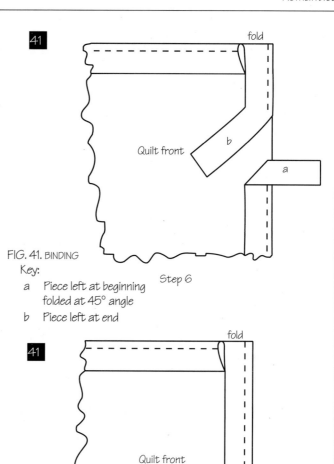

FIG. 41. BINDING

Step 4

FIG. 41. BINDING
Key:
  a Piece left
     at beginning
  b Piece left at end

FIG. 41. BINDING
Key:
  a Piece left at beginning
     folded at 45° angle
  b Piece left at end

FIG. 41. BINDING
Key:
  a Piece left at beginning and folded
  b Piece left at end and sewn in place

1. Make a fabric label, indicating the quilt name ROMANTICA or another name of your choice, your own name, the date, and any other information you think future generations may like to know.

If you iron freezer paper on the back of your label before writing on it, you'll find you can write with ease, especially if you use a sandpaper board under it. Remove the paper backing before attaching the label to your quilt.

A Sharpie® pen has permanent ink and is easy to use when writing on fabric. Consider decorating the label with your logo or with Jacobean flowers, using a Pigma Micron pen, which comes in a range of colors. Magic Sizing keeps a Pilot SC-UF pen from bleeding, if you'd like to use that. Some quiltmakers have success using the typewriter, word processor, or computer printer for the label information.

2. Heat set the label with a dry iron.

3. Stitch the label onto the back of your quilt.

4. Take a photograph of your quilt for your scrapbook and for insurance purposes.

5. Show ROMANTICA with pride. You have created a family heirloom.

EXOTICA intrigues;
ROMANTICA enthralls.

CHAPTER VI — COMPETITION

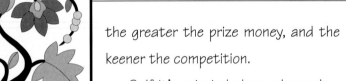

COMPETITION

Quiltmakers as well as athletes face judges, replays, Monday morning quarterbacks, and revel in accolades, awards, and adulation for a performance well done.

Pick up any quilt magazine and you'll see an announcement of a contest of some type somewhere some time. A prize is offered. Your interest is piqued.

Juried shows are becoming more and more popular. The judges are often internationally known. The competition is greater each year. The prizes are bigger, the publicity more rewarding.

This chapter is designed to help you avoid frustration, anger, and disappointment, should you decide to enter a contest.

DO YOUR HOMEWORK

Learn everything you can about the reputation of the show itself, about companies offering the prizes, and about the judges involved. Ask yourself some questions:

1. How big is the show? The bigger the show, the greater the prize money, and the keener the competition.

2. If it's a juried show, who makes up the jury?

3. What product does the company sponsor sell? If there is space on the entry blank, indicate that you used their product (if you did).

4. Who has won awards at past shows? For what kind of quilts?

5. If it's a judged show, who are the judges?

6. What are their likes and dislikes? Personal tastes? Prejudices?

Remember, companies are looking for good advertising material and judges are looking for ways to eliminate quilts. You may want to make a quilt that will fit a particular company's expectations or a specific judge's taste. Of course, it's okay to enter for the sole purpose of getting critiquéd.

CHECK YOUR QUILT, PRETENDING YOU ARE A JUDGE

Ask yourself the following questions:

1. Is my quilt squeaky clean (no pencil marks, fingerprints, blood, food stains, animal hair, or stale odors)?

2. Does the quilt have visual impact?

3. Is there color harmony? Balance?

4. Are the appliqué stitches fine with no puckering? Do any stitches show? Does the thread shade match the design fabric?

5. Are the circles round?

6. Are the points sharp?

7. Do any threads "eek" out?

8. Are the design pieces on grain with the background? If not, write an explanation on your entry form: "The pieces are not on grain with the background fabric. This has been done on purpose for additional texture."

9. Is there sufficient quilting? Not enough quilting is a common complaint of judges. Are the stitches consistent, small, the same size on both sides? Is the marking visible? Are there any knots showing? Are the straight lines of quilting evenly spaced? Does the quilting pattern complement the design?

10. Is the binding straight, not wavy? Is it the same width all around, front and back? Square at the corners? No stitches showing? The joinings true? The ending hidden? Does it relate to the quilt in terms of color, texture, and width?

11. Does the batting extend to the edge of the binding without lumping?

12. Is the quilt straight with no puckering, distortion, stretching, or waving? Check this out by hanging the quilt; don't just lay it out on a bed or on the floor. Usually a photo of your *hanging* quilt is a requirement for entry.

FILL OUT THE ENTRY FORM NEATLY AND COMPLETELY

This is self-explanatory. A sample of an AQS entry form appears on page 159. It is typical and can serve as a model.

Be True to the Theme

Be obvious in your quilt so that no one misses the connection between your treatment and the theme.

Follow the Rules Exactly

Consider every statement on the entry form highly significant, no matter how unimportant you think it might be. For example, if there are minimum and maximum measurements required, slavishly follow them. Wouldn't it be tragic if the finest quilt in the whole world were disqualified because it measured 1" (2.5 cm) too narrow?

Make Good Slides

Often the entry form will give you some pointers on what makes a good photo and what kind of a photo is expected. Pay attention.

Mailing

1. Be sure your quilt is labeled with a fabric label stitched to the back of the quilt including: the name of the quilt, your name, address, and phone number.

2. Fold your quilt carefully and wrap it in acid free tissue paper. Place the wrapped quilt in a plastic bag to protect it against dampness. Also, cover the quilt with a sheet of cardboard for protection when box is cut open.

3. Pack it in a strong box. Label the destination and the source clearly.

4. The size of the box should be adequate to hold the quilt — not so small you have to squish the quilt or so large that the box could be smashed during shipping.

5. Enclose a self addressed stamped postcard for acknowledgment of receipt of the quilt. Type or print on the reverse side: the name of the quilt, your name, date received, signature, and position of the person signing for the quilt.

6. Insure the package.

OTHER COMMENTS

Under no circumstances copy an original design and claim it as original or "my design." If it is copyrighted (as ROMANTICA is), this is illegal. If you change some aspect of the design, you can say "this is an adaptation of..." or "this was inspired by..." and give the person's name (in this case, Patricia B. Campbell) and the name of the design. Giving credit to the designer does not diminish your creation.

Unfortunately, you need to be aware of some negatives regarding quilt competitions. In many shows team quilts (for example, one person appliqués and another quilts) and group quilts (a number of people do the top and quilting) are lumped together, which is often a disadvantage. Some judges look for original designs only. An exquisitely executed quilt may be passed over, if it is noticeable that it has been done from a workshop or a popular book.

Always enter a contest with the expectation of winning. However, if you do not win, you still reap the benefit of having the judges' critiques. Therefore, do not hesitate to enter.

A ribbon mentality is easy to acquire. It feels so good. Viewers respond with compliments. Writers seek you out for articles. Magazines ask to picture your creation on their covers. Quiltmakers recognize you and your work. Prizes are fun to receive. A money award is intoxicating. Your home gets decorated with what amounts to a quilter's loving cup and you get to show off your ribbons and other awards with pride to family, friends, and casual visitors. If you aren't interested in seeking awards, you can bask in the sunshine of praise from everyone who sees your treasure. Go for it!

Look again at the photos in the book — the featured quilt ROMANTICA and the students' versions of ROMANTICA — and look at yours. Isn't it amazing that seven wall quilts all made from the same pattern would each reflect the individual personality and the creative spirit of the quiltmaker!

Quiltmakers are like athletes — they love planning their moves, revel in playing the game, and delight in winning.

ROMANTICA

PATTERN &
COLOR PLATE
SECTION

ROMANTICA- BLOCK #1
Stitched by Ruth Kock, Port Elizabeth, South Africa

Romantica

BLOCK #1
Upper Left Quadrant

center line

bias

AA

BB

25

Y

24

DD

21

W

23

U

22

CC

21

FF

26

GG

17

EE

21

Z

20

14

I

V

18

X

19

center line

bias

60

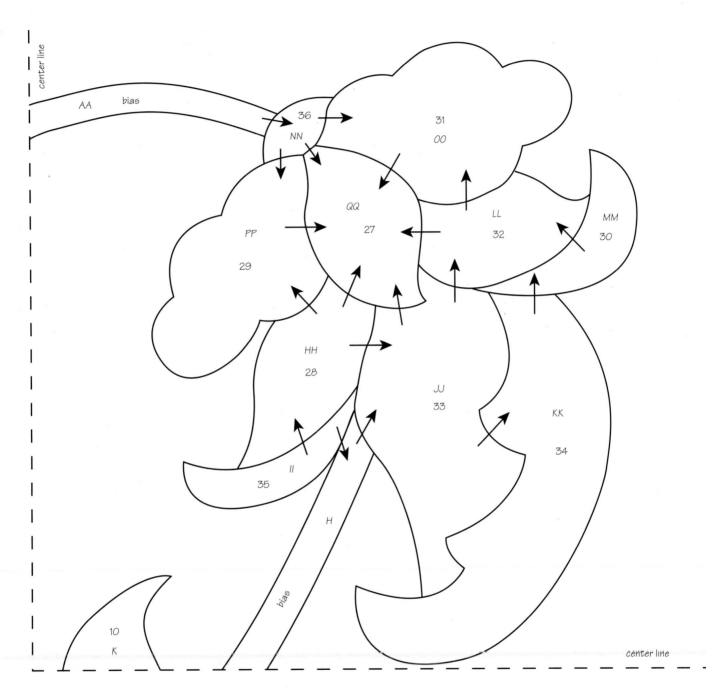

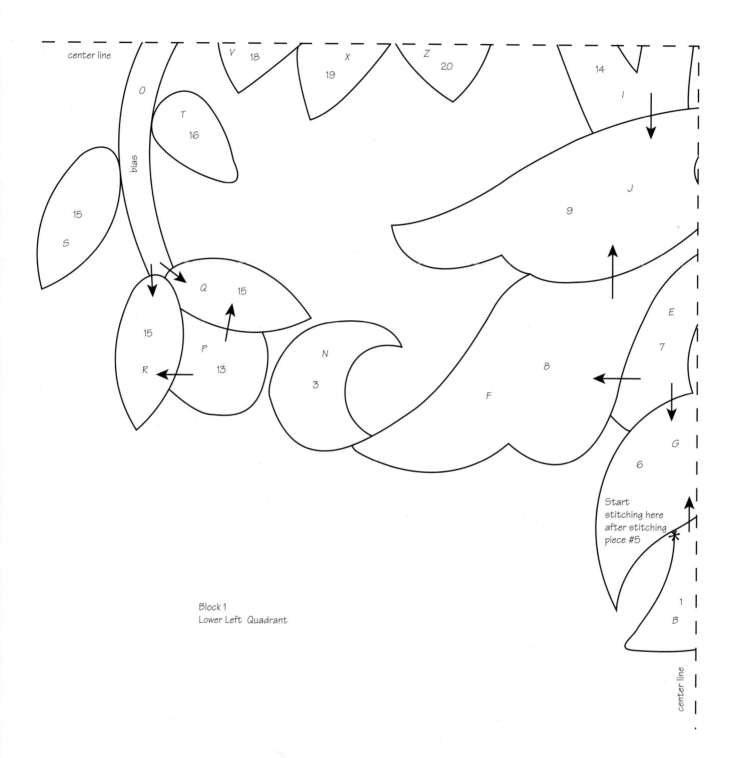

center line

V 18

X

Z 20

19

14

O

bias

T 16

I

J

15

S

9

Q

15

15

P

R

13

N

3

E

7

8

F

G

6

Start stitching here after stitching piece #5

1

B

Block 1
Lower Left Quadrant

center line

BLOCK #1
Lower Left Quadrant

BLOCK #1
Lower Right Quadrant

ROMANTICA - BLOCK #2
Stitched by Arletha L. Raymond, Fremont, California

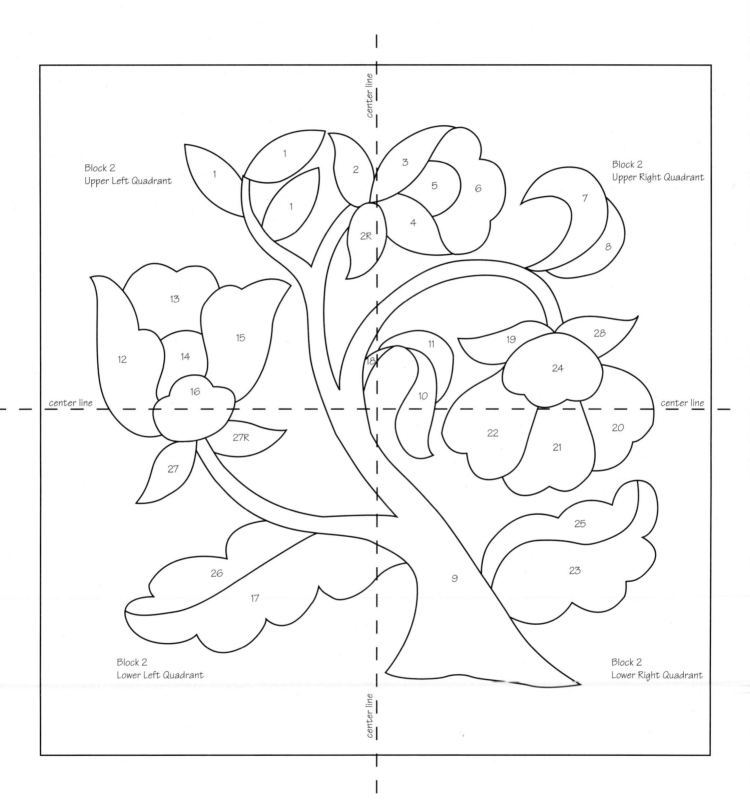

Block 2
Upper Left Quadrant

Block 2
Upper Right Quadrant

center line

center line

center line

center line

Block 2
Lower Left Quadrant

Block 2
Lower Right Quadrant

BLOCK #2
Upper Left Quadrant

BLOCK #2
Upper Right Quadrant

center line

3

5

6

7

4

2R

8

9

28

11

19

18

24

10

22

20

21

center line

67

Romantica

center line

12

16

27R

27

9

9

26

17

center line

BLOCK #2
Lower Left Quadrant

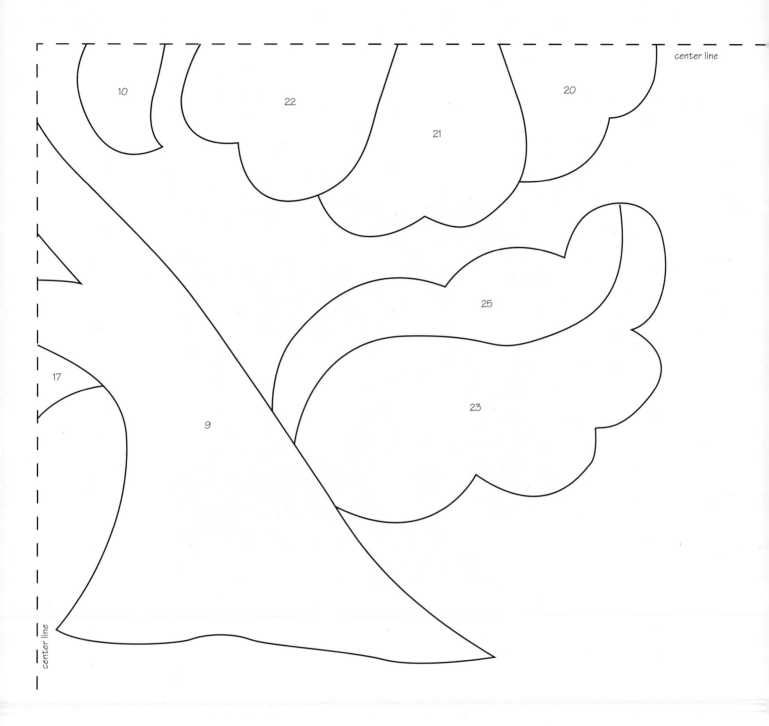

center line

10

22

21

20

center line

25

17

9

23

center line

BLOCK #2
Lower Right Quadrant

ROMANTICA - BLOCK #3
Stitched by Jo Quiram, Plainview, Minnesota

Block 3
Upper Left Quadrant

Block 3
Upper Right Quadrant

bias

bias

13

12

10

10

center line

7

1

1

8

1

9

1

9

1

9

bias

center line

center line

1

1

9

16

1

6

4

1

2

3

1

5

15

1

bias

14

11

Block 3
Lower Left Quadrant

Block 3
Lower Right Quadrant

center line

BLOCK #3
Upper Left Quadrant

center line

center line

BLOCK #3
Upper Right Quadrant

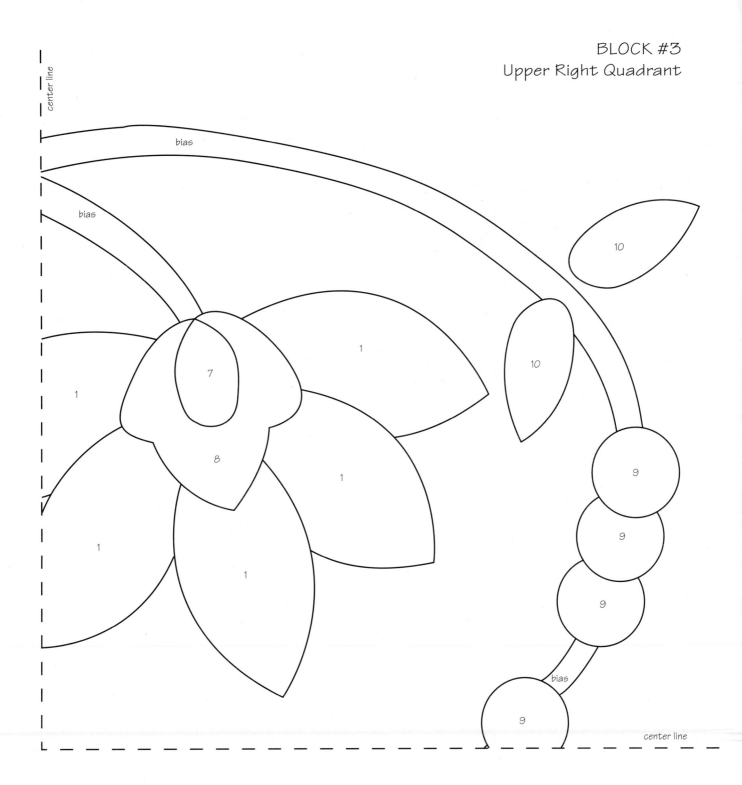

center line

1

1

14

1

6

4

2

3

5

1

1

14

center line

BLOCK #3
Lower Left Quadrant

center line

9

16

center line

bias

14

15

11

BLOCK #3
Lower Right Quadrant

ROMANTICA- BLOCK #4
Stitched by Jan Schulz, Austin, Minnesota

Block 4
Upper Left Quadrant

Block 4
Upper Right Quadrant

center line

center line

center line

center line

Block 4
Lower Left Quadrant

Block 4
Lower Right Quadrant

bias

bias

bias

BLOCK #4
Upper Left Quadrant

BLOCK #4
Upper Right Quadrant

center line

bias

12

12

11

11

11

11

11

11

11

11

11

10

9

9R

6

8

center line

center line

12   12

6

11   11

11   11

11

11   11

11

11

10

9R

9   1

BLOCK #4
Lower Left Quadrant

center line

center line

9

9R

6

8

7

6

4

4

5

5

10

3

5

9R

2

5

4

4

1

center line

BLOCK #4
Lower Right Quadrant

ROMANTICA - BLOCK #5
Stitched by Sally Barnes, Manhattan Beach, California

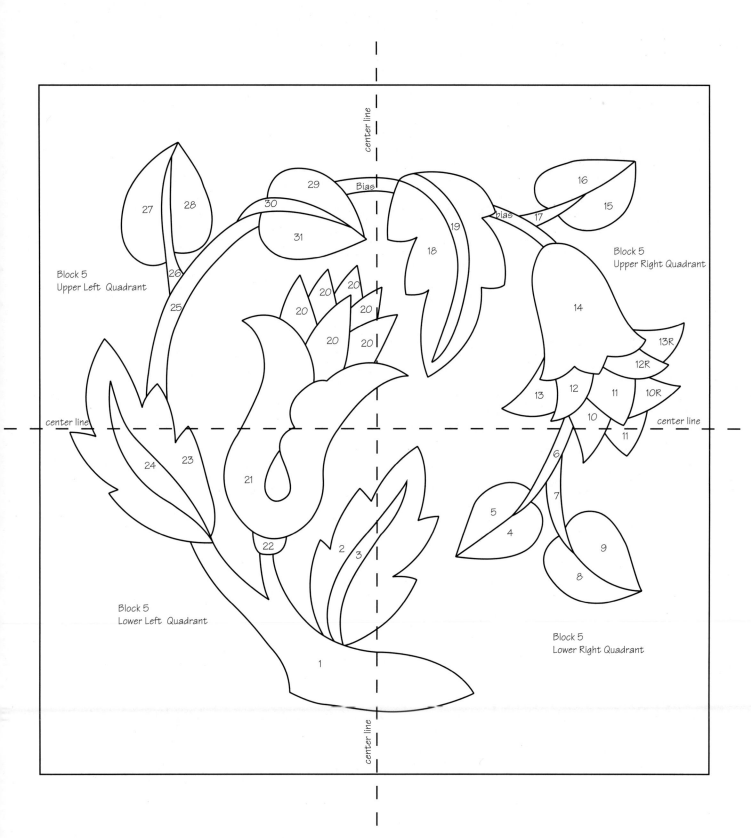

Block 5
Upper Left Quadrant

Block 5
Upper Right Quadrant

center line

center line

Block 5
Lower Left Quadrant

Block 5
Lower Right Quadrant

center line

center line

Bias

bias

83

BLOCK #5
Upper Left Quadrant

center line

bias

29

30

27

28

31

26

20

20

25

20

20

20

20

21

Tulip template on page 150.

24

23

center line

BLOCK #5
Upper Right Quadrant

center line

bias

bias

16

15

17

19

18

14

20

20

13R

12R

21

12

11

10R

13

10

11

6

center line

center line

24

23

21

Tulip template on page 150.

22

2

3

1

center line

BLOCK #5
Lower Left Quadrant

center line

center line

center line

1

2

3

4

5

6

7

8

9

10

11

BLOCK #5
Lower Right Quadrant

ROMANTICA - BLOCK #6
Stitched by Marsha S. Dardenne, St. Francisville, Louisiana

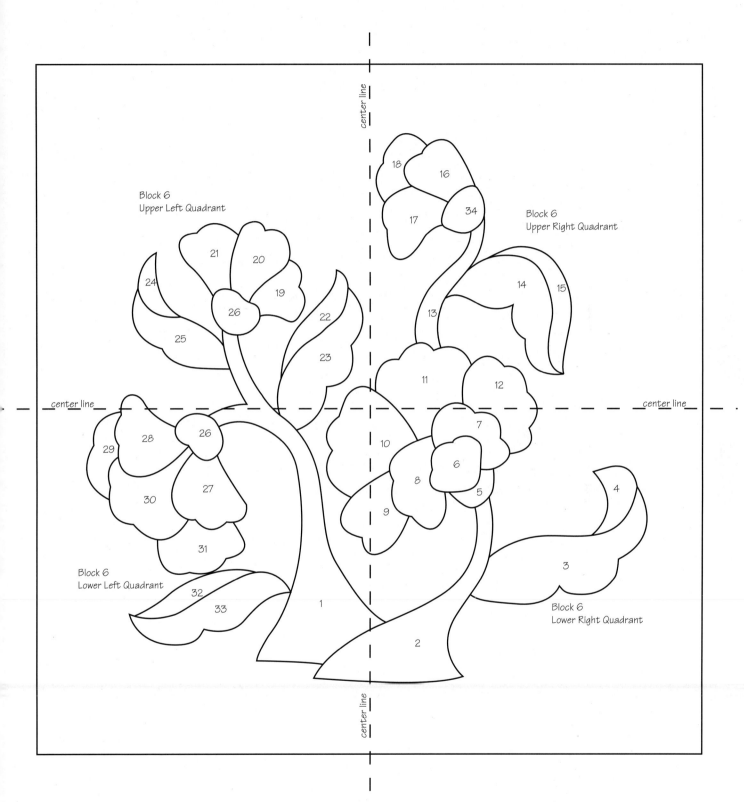

Block 6
Upper Left Quadrant

Block 6
Upper Right Quadrant

center line

center line

Block 6
Lower Left Quadrant

Block 6
Lower Right Quadrant

BLOCK #6
Upper Left Quadrant

BLOCK #6
Upper Right Quadrant

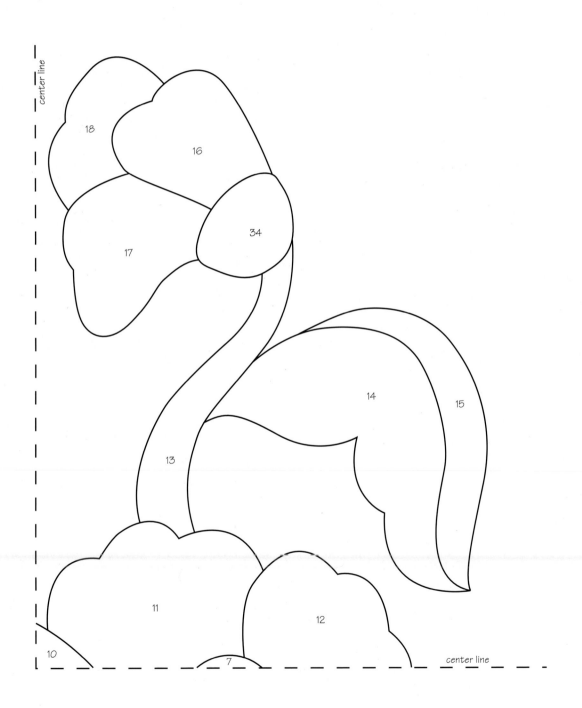

center line

18

16

17

34

14

15

13

11

12

10

7

center line

center line

23

26

28

29

10

30

27

9

31

32

33

1

2

center line

BLOCK #6
Lower Left Quadrant

center line

11

7

12

10

6

8

5

4

9

3

1

2

center line

BLOCK #6
Lower Right Quadrant

ROMANTICA- BLOCK #7
Stitched by Cyndee Brown, Baton Rouge, Louisiana

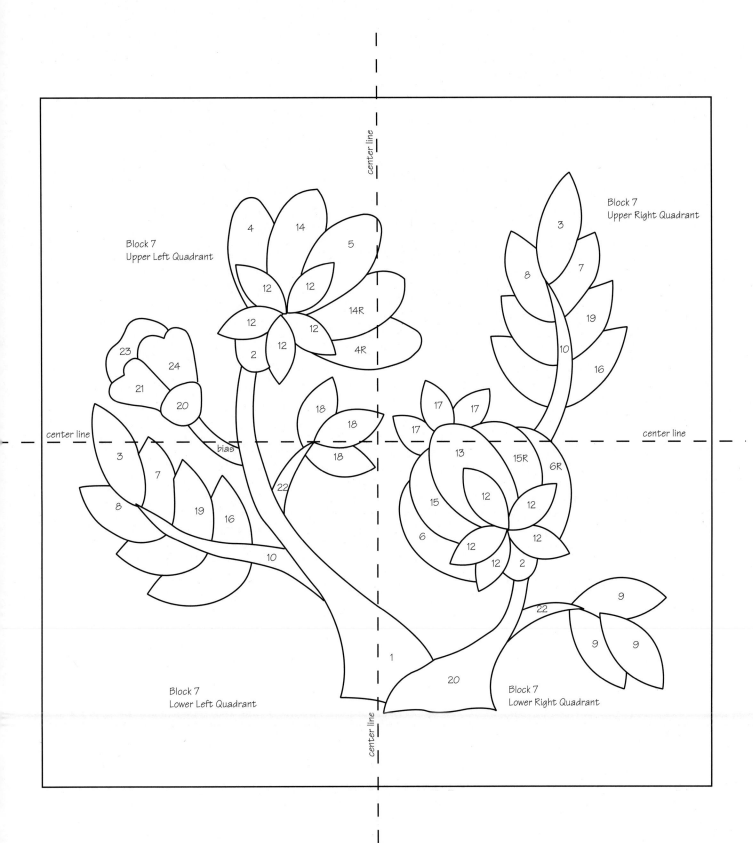

Block 7
Upper Left Quadrant

Block 7
Upper Right Quadrant

center line

center line

center line

bias

Block 7
Lower Left Quadrant

Block 7
Lower Right Quadrant

center line

BLOCK #7
Upper Left Quadrant

BLOCK #7
Upper Right Quadrant

center line

center line

5

14R

4R

3

7

8

19

10

16

17

17

17

13

15R

6R

97

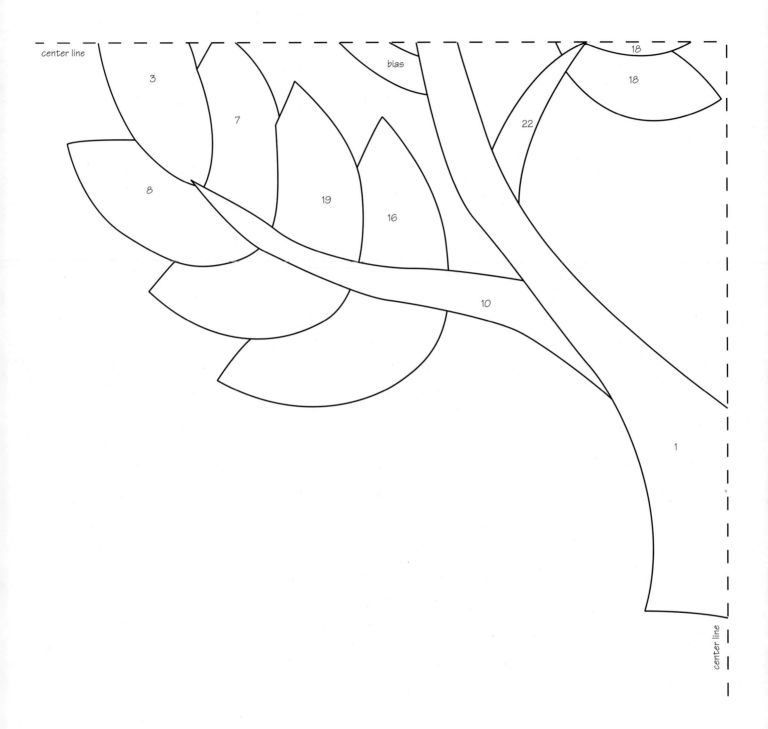

center line

3

7

bias

18

18

22

8

19

16

10

1

center line

BLOCK #7
Lower Left Quadrant

center line

center line

17

13

15R

6R

12

15

12

6

12

12

12

12

2

9

22

9

9

1

20

BLOCK #7
Lower Right Quadrant

ROMANTICA - BLOCK #8
Stitched by Mae Marrs Luigs, Garland, Texas

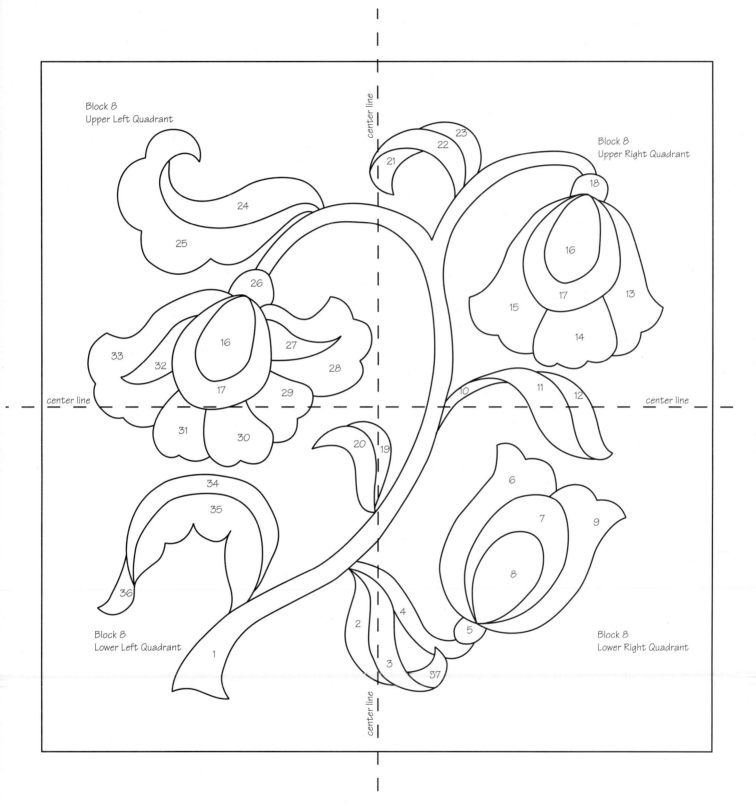

Block 8
Upper Left Quadrant

center line

Block 8
Upper Right Quadrant

center line

center line

Block 8
Lower Left Quadrant

center line

Block 8
Lower Right Quadrant

BLOCK #8
Upper Left Quadrant

center line

center line

22

21

24

1

25

26

16

27

33

32

28

17

31

29

30

BLOCK #8
Upper Right Quadrant

center line

center line

center line

33

31

30

29

19

20

34

35

36

4

2

3

1

canter line

BLOCK #8
Lower Left Quadrant

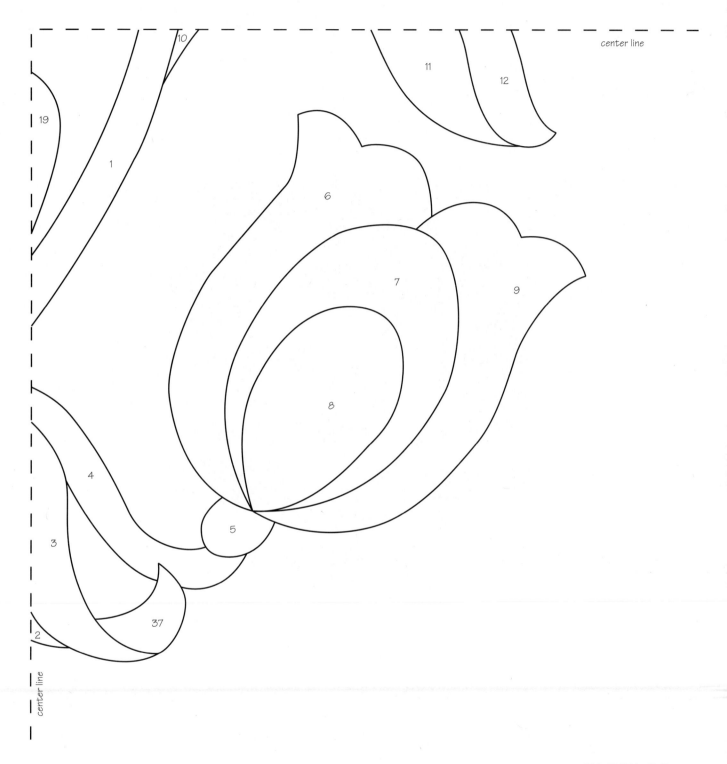

center line

19

10

1

11

12

6

7

9

8

4

3

5

37

2

center line

BLOCK #8
Lower Right Quadrant

ROMANTICA - BLOCK #9
Stitched by Pam Goldkorn, Durban, South Africa

Block 9
Upper Left Quadrant

Block 9
Upper Right Quadrant

center line

center line

bias

Block 9
Lower Right Quadrant

Block 9
Lower Left Quadrant

center line

center line

BLOCK #9
Upper Left Quadrant

center line

center line

BLOCK #9
Upper Right Quadrant

center line

30

31

32

30

34

33

30

25

25

25

25

25

25

25

bias

11

9

10

8

7

7

7

6

17

16

13

14

27

2

5

center line

center line

24

23

19

18

14

15

22

22

bias

22

21

20

1

2

center line

BLOCK #9
Lower Left Quadrant

14

13

27

center line

15

12

4

3

1

2

center line

BLOCK #9
Lower Right Quadrant

ROMANTICA- BLOCK #10
Stitched by Shiona Clark, Port Elizabeth, South Africa

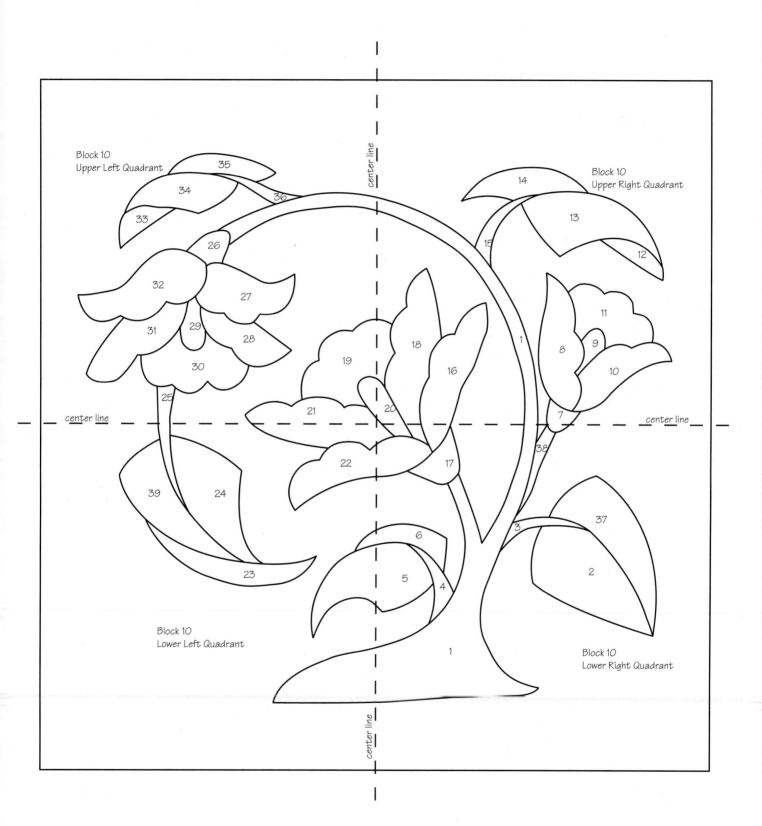

Block 10
Upper Left Quadrant

35

34

36

33

26

32

27

31 29 28

30

25

center line

39 24

23

Block 10
Lower Left Quadrant

center line

19

21 20

22 17

center line

18

16

14

Block 10
Upper Right Quadrant

13

15

12

11

8 9

1 10

7

38

3 37

6

5 4

2

1

Block 10
Lower Right Quadrant

center line

center line

BLOCK #10
Upper Left Quadrant

BLOCK #10
Upper Right Quadrant

center line

25

21

22

39

24

6

5

23

1

center line

BLOCK #10
Lower Left Quadrant

center line

21 20 18 16

22 17

38

7

37

3

6

5 4

2

1

center line

BLOCK #10
Lower Right Quadrant

ROMANTICA - BLOCK #11
Stitched by Kathy Jardine, Dublin, California

Block 11
Upper Left Quadrant

Block 11
Upper Right Quadrant

center line

center line

center line

center line

Block 11
Lower Left Quadrant

Block 11
Lower Right Quadrant

bias

bias

BLOCK #11
Upper Left Quadrant

center line

center line

bias

center line

7

6

6

7

23

5

4

11

10

2

3

1

center line

BLOCK #11
Lower Left Quadrant

center line

23

17R

20

17

18

15

16R

16

24

19

14

11

10

13

1

12

center line

BLOCK #11
Lower Right Quadrant

ROMANTICA - BLOCK #12
Stitched by Beryl Healy, Port Elizabeth, South Africa

BLOCK #12
Upper Left Quadrant

BLOCK #12
Upper Right Quadrant

center line

center line

center line

37

16

16

16

14

15

38

39

6

1

center line

BLOCK #12
Lower Left Quadrant

16

center line

12

13

11

10

4

14

15

9

3

14

8

7

6

2

1

center line

BLOCK #12
Lower Right Quadrant

ROMANTICA - BOTTOM BORDER (ROTATE FOR TOP BORDER)
Bottom border stitched by Ina Ericson, Richardson, Texas
Top border stitched by Pam Goldkorn, Durban, South Africa

Top

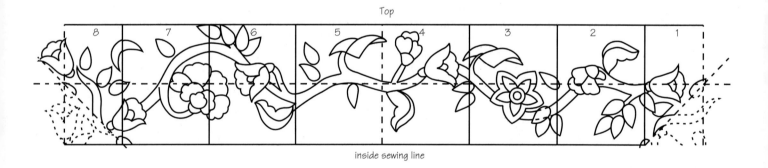

inside sewing line

Bottom

inside sewing line

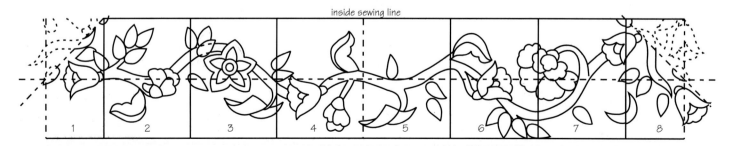

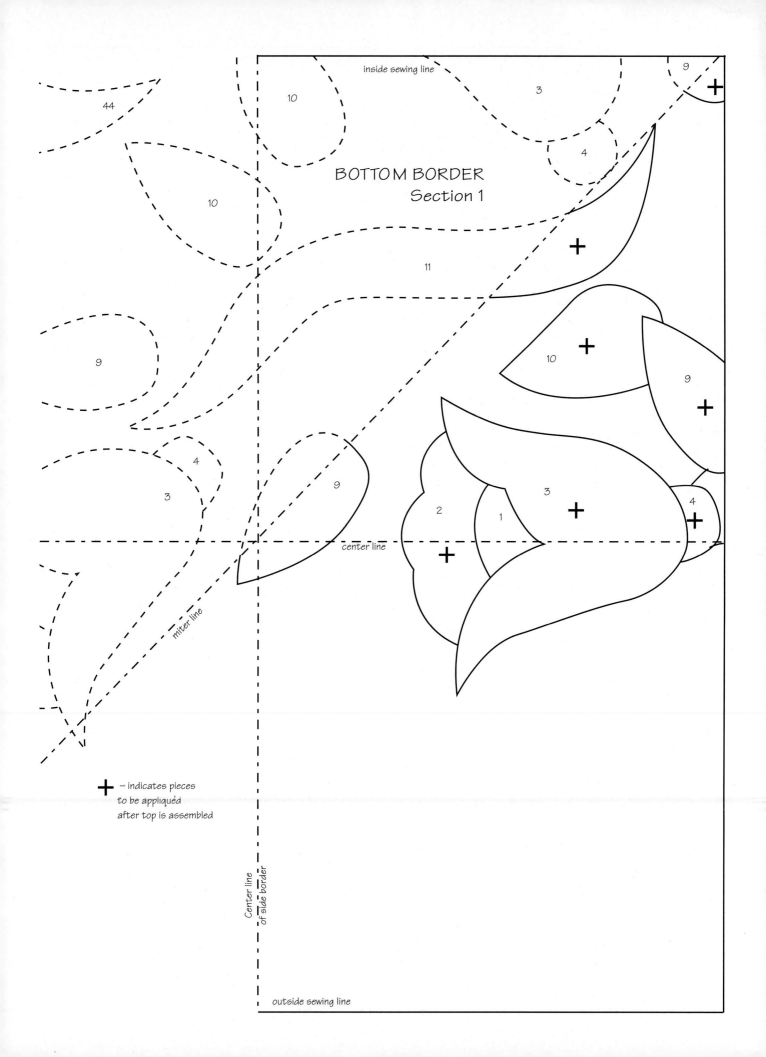

44

10

inside sewing line

10

3

9

4

BOTTOM BORDER
Section 1

11

10

9

9

9

4

2   1   3   4

3

center line

miter line

✚ – indicates pieces
to be appliquéd
after top is assembled

Center line
of side border

outside sewing line

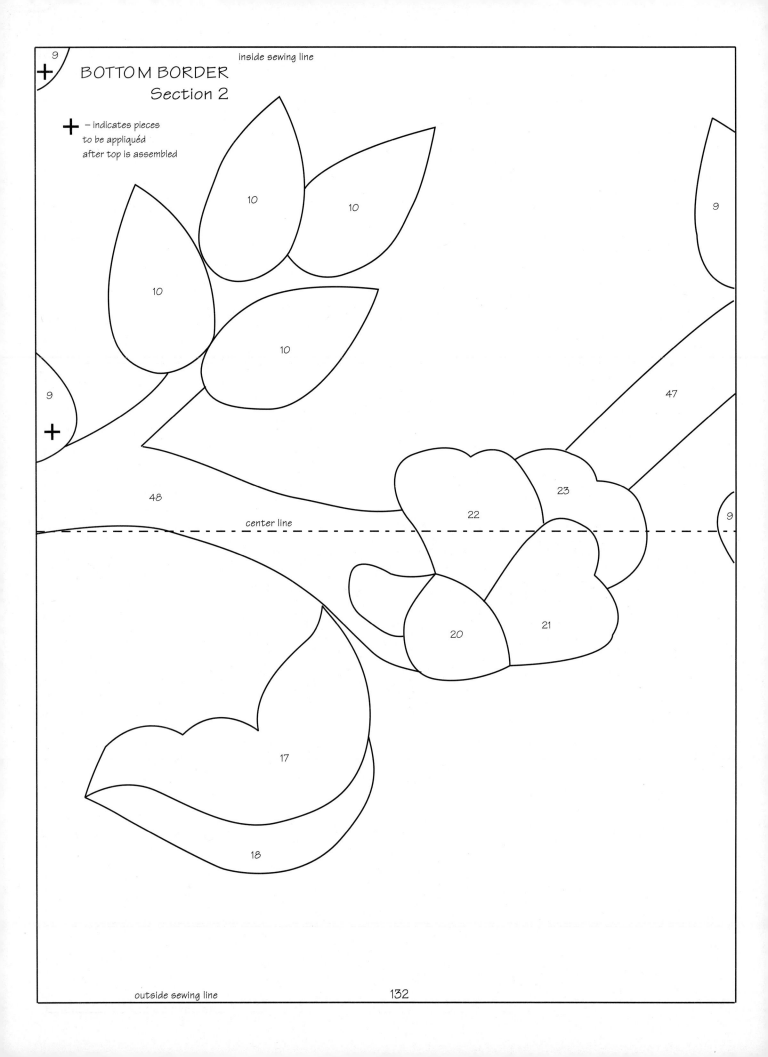

BOTTOM BORDER
Section 2

+ – indicates pieces
to be appliquéd
after top is assembled

9

10

10

10

10

10

9

9

9

47

48

center line

23

22

20

21

17

18

9

10

10

47

12 13 14

15

46

9

9

9

center line

6

7

8

BOTTOM BORDER
Section 4

18

17

9

9

45

center line

vertical center line

46

4

2   1   3

20

8

21

22

6

7

23

BOTTOM BORDER
Section 5

9

center line

45

vertical center line

9

10

7

8

6

outside sewing line

BOTTOM BORDER
Section 6

18

17

45

38

33

26

center line

27   28

37

25

36

24

43

10

10

10

10

10

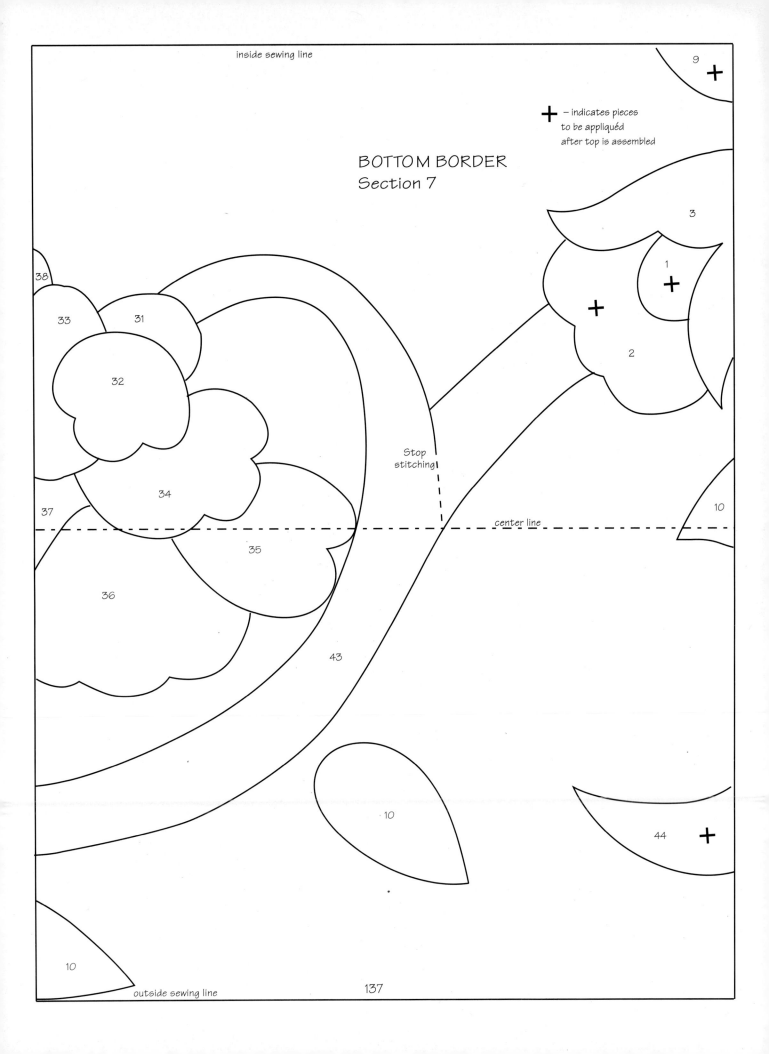

inside sewing line

+ — indicates pieces
to be appliquéd
after top is assembled

BOTTOM BORDER
Section 7

Stop
stitching

center line

outside sewing line

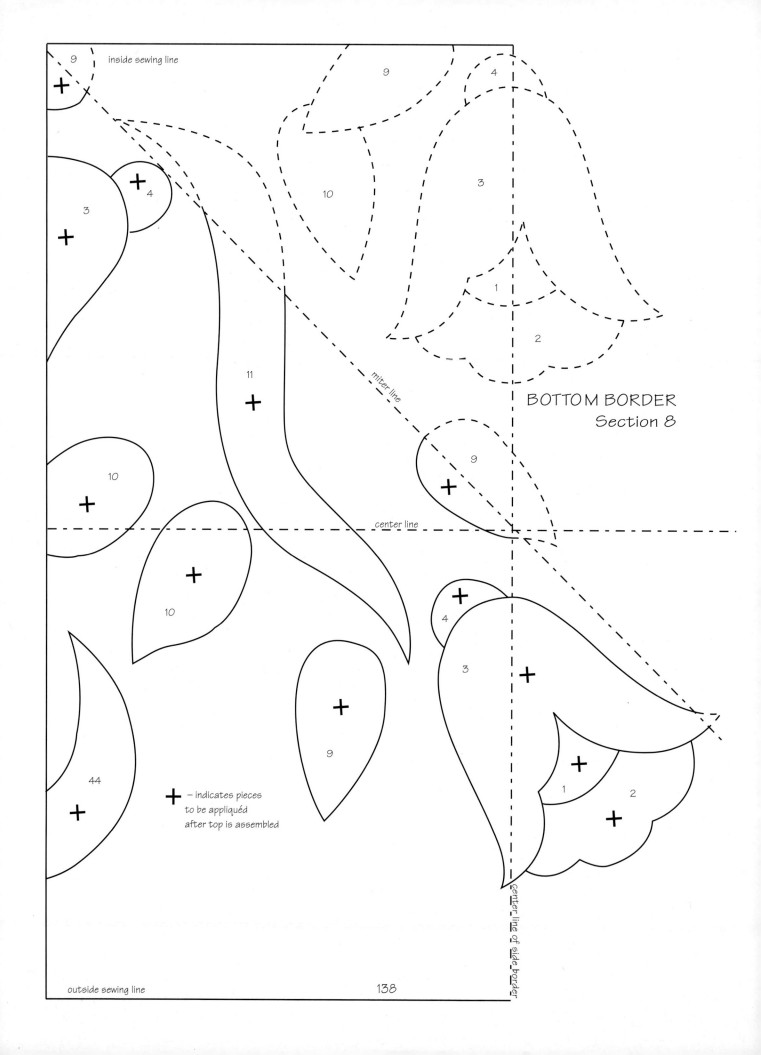

9

9

4

10

3

1

2

miter line

BOTTOM BORDER
Section 8

3

4

11

10

9

center line

10

4

3

10

9

+ – indicates pieces
to be appliquéd
after top is assembled

44

1

2

center line of side border

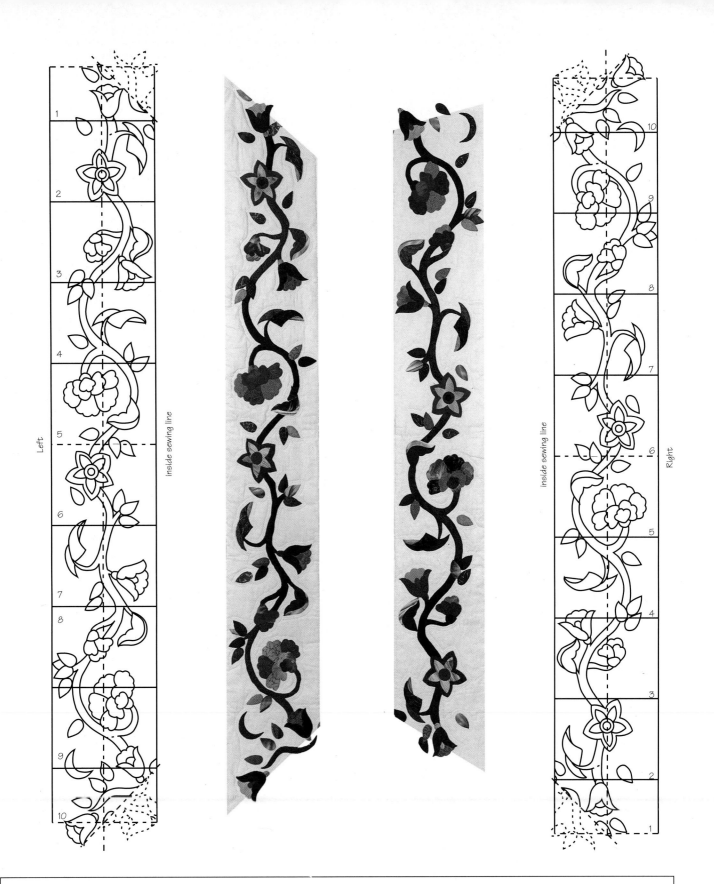

ROMANTICA - RIGHT BORDER (ROTATE FOR LEFT BORDER)
Right border stitched by Terry Monson, Roscoe, Illinois
Left border stitched by Stephania L. Bommarito, Torrance, California

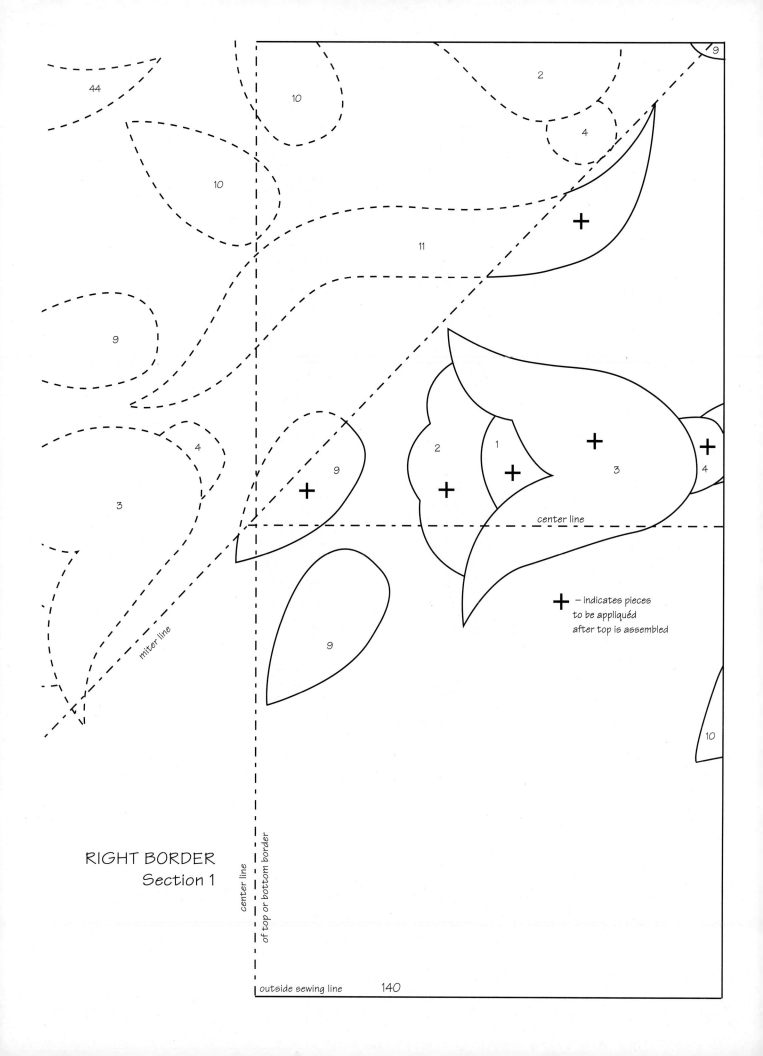

44

2

10

9

4

10

11

+

9

4

2

1

+

+

3

+

4

+

center line

9

+

3

+ – indicates pieces
to be appliquéd
after top is assembled

9

10

miter line

RIGHT BORDER
Section 1

center line
of top or bottom border

outside sewing line   140

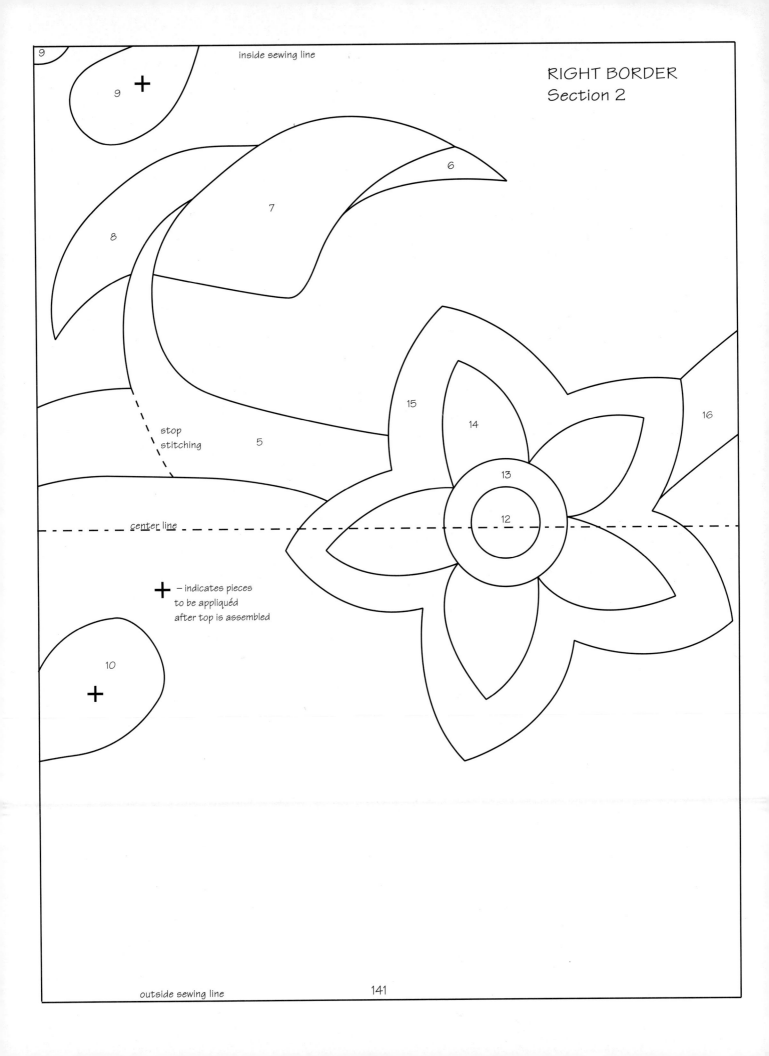

9

9

+

6

7

8

15

14

16

13

12

stop
stitching

5

center line

+ – indicates pieces
to be appliquéd
after top is assembled

10

+

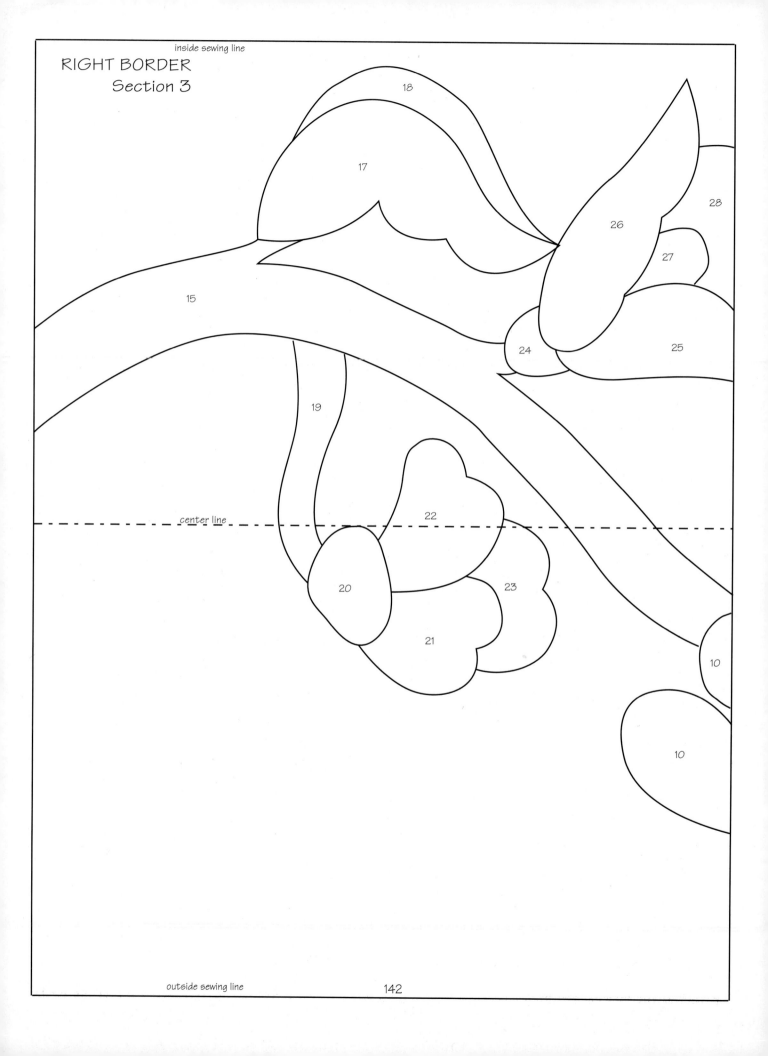

RIGHT BORDER
Section 5

RIGHT BORDER
Section 6

10

10

10

10

10

42

center line

41

15

14

13

12

9

6

7

vertical center line

RIGHT BORDER
Section 7

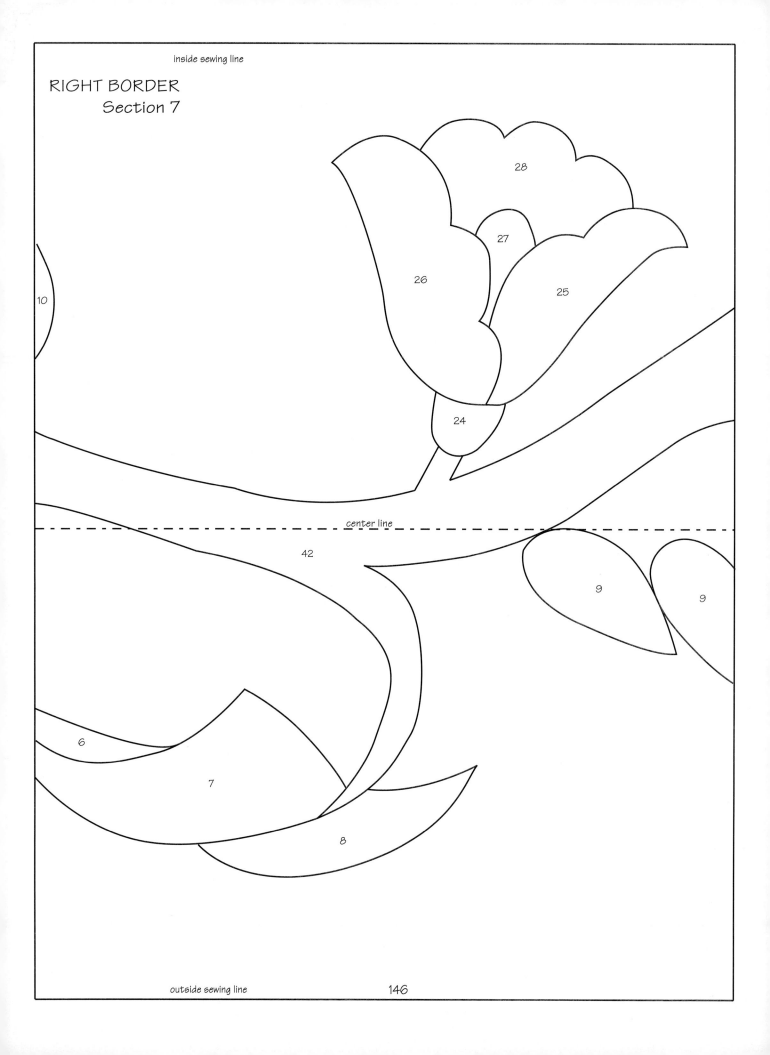

28

27

26

25

24

10

center line

42

9

9

6

7

8

center line

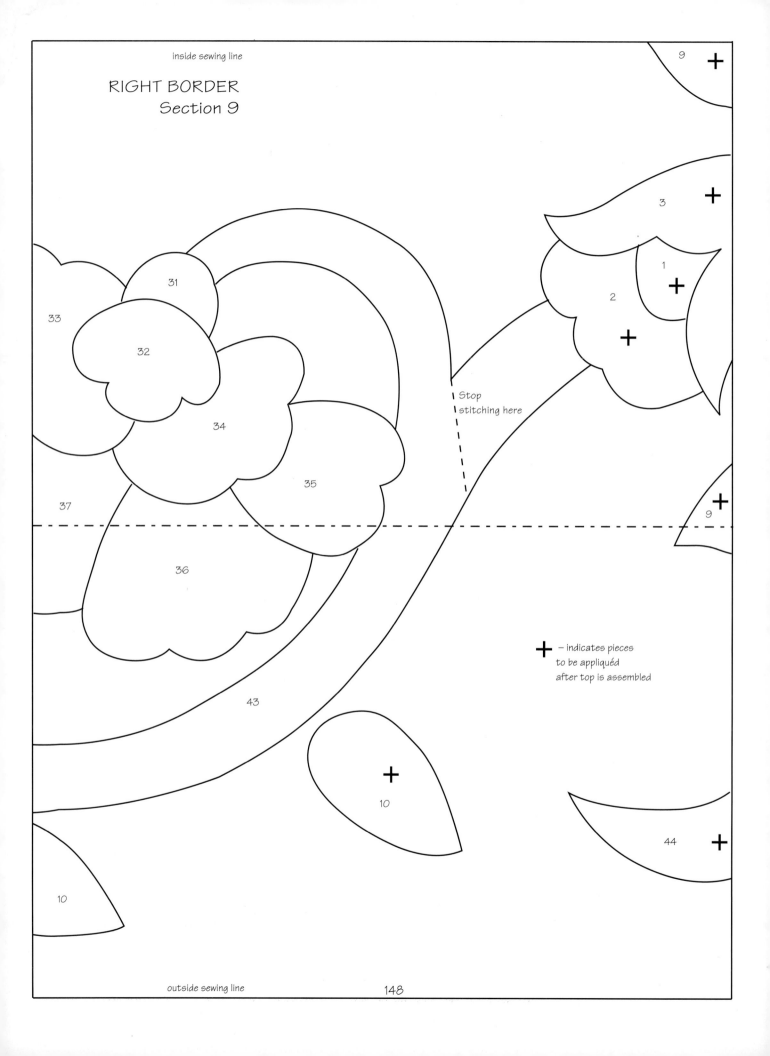

RIGHT BORDER
Section 9

9

3

1

2

Stop
stitching here

31

33

32

34

35

37

9

36

43

– indicates pieces
to be appliquéd
after top is assembled

10

44

10

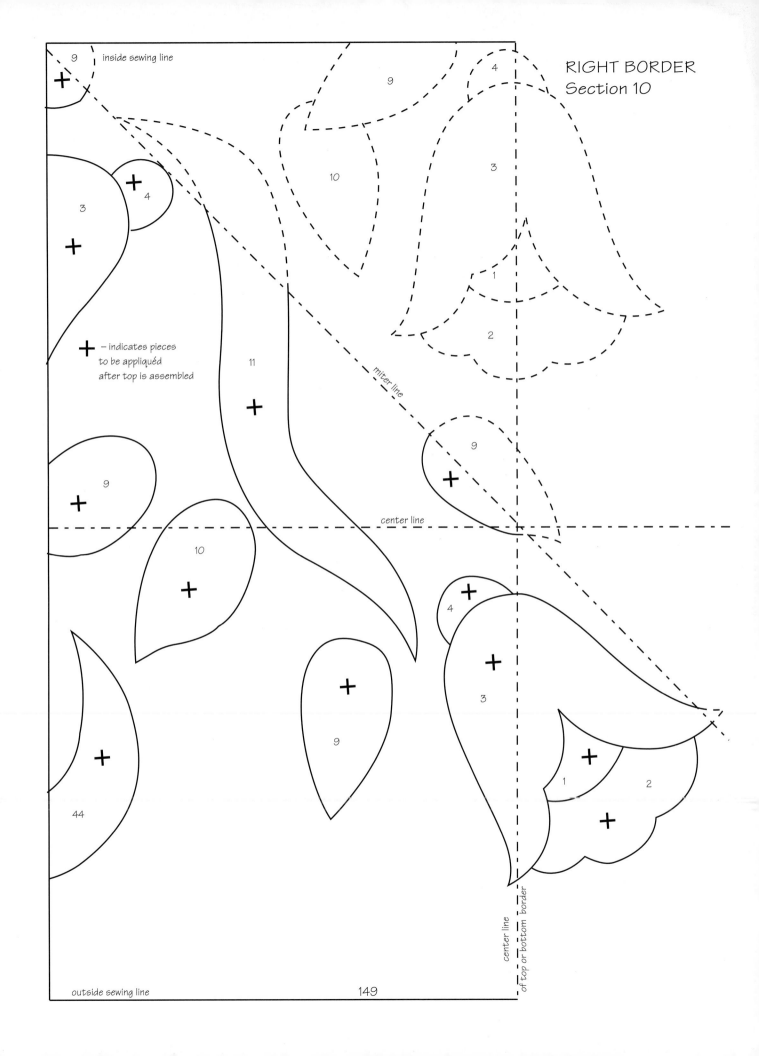

9   inside sewing line

RIGHT BORDER
Section 10

9

4

10

9

3

3   4

1

2

+ – indicates pieces
to be appliquéd
after top is assembled

11

miter line

9

9

center line

10

4

3

9

44

1   2

center line
of top or bottom border

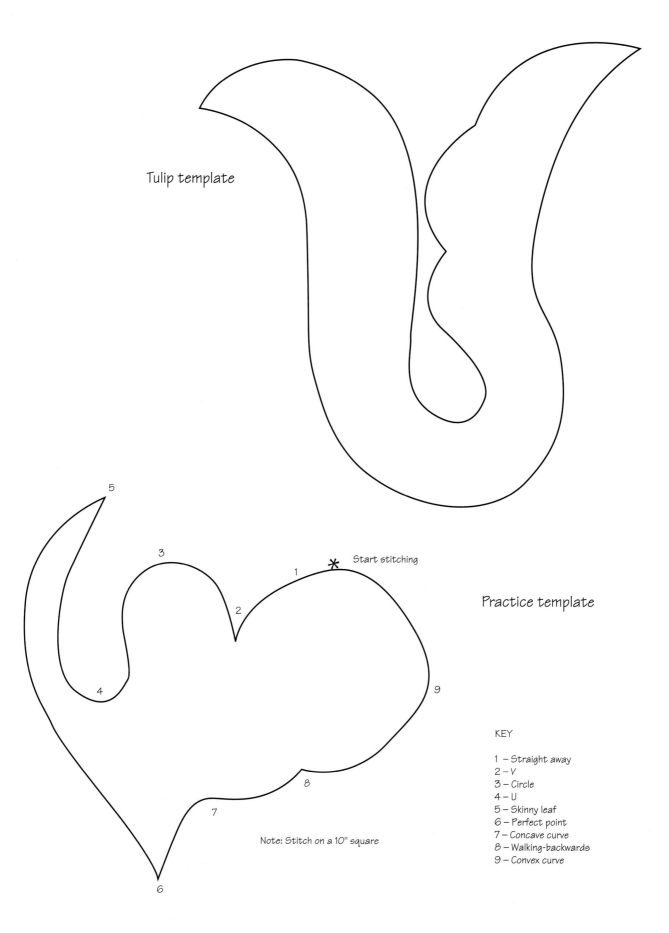

Tulip template

Start stitching

Practice template

Note: Stitch on a 10" square

KEY

1 – Straight away
2 – V
3 – Circle
4 – U
5 – Skinny leaf
6 – Perfect point
7 – Concave curve
8 – Walking-backwards
9 – Convex curve

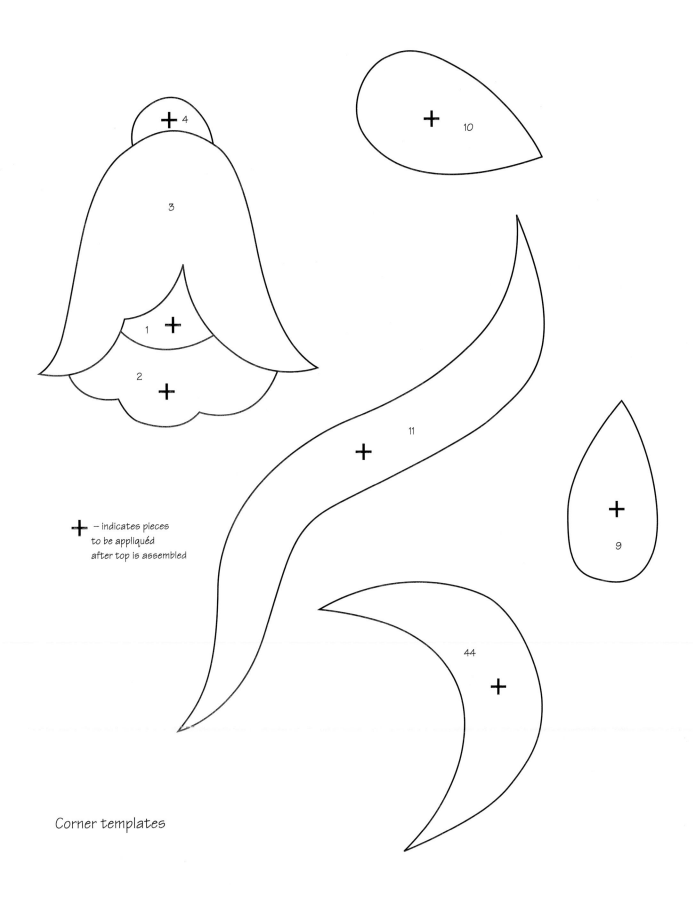

4

3

10

1

2

11

+ — indicates pieces
   to be appliquéd
   after top is assembled

9

44

Corner templates

ANSWERS TO THE QUESTIONS MOST OFTEN ASKED

Q. What makes a Jacobean quilt different from other quilts?

A. Jacobean quilt characteristics are: designs from crewel embroidery, a wide palette of colors, appliqué exclusive of embellishment, botanical fantasy rather than realism, and hidden rather than emphasized stitches.

Q. Should I always use 100% cotton fabric?

A. Cotton is the easiest fabric to work with, but try others. Experiment. Resist-print cottons are often hard to needle. Wool, linen, velvet are heavy. Rayon and blends are hard to needle turn. Silk flattens when pressed.

Q. How do I know if a piece of fabric in my collection is 100% cotton?

A. Snip off a small piece, put it in an ashtray and set it on fire. If ashes of the "blow-away" type remain, it's 100% cotton. Another reaction, such as melting, indicates that synthetic fibers are present.

Q. Should I wash and iron the fabric before cutting?

A. It's up to you. A quilt used as a wall hanging will get less soiled than a bed quilt. You can have the quilt dry cleaned. The colors then stay bright, the fabric crisp, and you don't have to spend time prewashing the fabric.

Q. Can I use all solid color fabrics?

A. Solids tend to look flat. If you decide to use solids, use all solids with no prints.

Q. Can I use printed background fabric?

A. Yes, if the print is subtle.

Q. What about tone-on-tone fabric?

A. Great, but be cautious about resist prints as they may be difficult to needle.

Q. Isn't it hard to stitch on a black background?

A. No, because you're stitching on the design fabric, rather than the background.

Q. Is the tree trunk always only one fabric?

A. It can be one or several. Try the leaf shading technique.

Q. What about the fabric in the center of the tulip? There is no template for it.

A. It's a rectangle tucked underneath. See page 30.

Q. Doesn't photocopying distort a pattern?

A. Yes, but minimally. It doesn't matter. There is freedom in appliqué not found in piecing.

Q. Where can I purchase a grease pencil?

A. Quilt shops, craft and office supply stores.

Q. Should I mark the background fabric?

A. You can, but you don't have to. Instructions for marking minimally are on page 26 and instructions on avoiding marking are on page 27.

Q. Should I lay the template on the straight, on the bias, or does it matter?

A. Use the bias as much as possible because it eases the needle turning and there is less fraying.

Q. Do I cut out all the pieces for the block before I start to stitch?

A. Yes. You want to look at the block composition as a whole, checking for harmony and balance.

Q. What kind of lamp is best?

A. A table gooseneck works well for trying out fabrics and laying out pieces. A pendant lamp helps for stitching. Make sure the light bulb wattage is high enough to see well. A 72W halogen bulb is bright and cool.

Q. Should I baste?

A. As little as possible. Only very large pieces such as the tree trunks may need to be thread basted to keep them from shifting. If basting makes you less anxious, pin the other pieces, putting the pins on the back side.

Q. What thread should I use?

A. Mettler #60 machine embroidery; #50 DMC machine embroidery; #50 all other brands, silk and rayon. Rayon comes in beautiful shades and has a sheen, but it untwists. Silk curls and is expensive.

Q. Where can I find this thread?

A. Some quilt shops. Viking, Bernina, Pfaff, and Singer Sewing Centers teach machine embroidery classes, so they carry it more often than do quilt shops.

Q. What is the best size and brand of needle?

A. #12 or #10 Betweens. Clover needles don't break or bend. John James needles bend. Piecemaker needles are thick.

Q. Must I use a short needle?

A. There are no musts, but since only ⅓ of the needle is needed for needle turn, why use a longer one that means more to push through the fabric. Also shorter is stronger.

Q. How about a platinum needle?

A. It's dull, fat, breaks, and is expensive.

Q. A gold needle?

A. It's fat; use a thin needle.

Q. Why can't I use my needle instead of a quilting pin for the perfect points?

A. The quilting pin is stronger and will do a better job.

Q. Which piece do I appliqué first?

A. Start with the tree trunk, which is usually your biggest piece. Make sure before you stitch that there are no pieces which need to go under it. If so, do the "under" pieces first.

Q. Where do I start stitching?

A. On a gentle curve or straight-away. Never start at a point.

Q. What size seam allowance do I use for appliqué?

A. ⅛" (3 mm) and when you feel comfortable with this, try 1/16" (1.5 mm).

Q. And what size seam allowance for sewing seams?

A. ¼" (6 mm).

Q. What do I use the various types of pins for?

A. Shashiko pins to pin pieces to the master pattern; sequin pins to hold circles and other small pieces in place until stitching is well started; quilting pins to make perfect points.

Q. Do I put the needle into the background directly out from where it comes up in the fold of the design piece?

A. Yes, see Fig. 22.

Q. How do I finish stitching?

A. With a knot on the back of the block, the tail tucked between the BF and DF away from the edge so the thread doesn't sneak out. See instructions on page 38.

Q. Should I clip the curve of a design piece?

A. Rarely, because the seam allowance is narrow, ⅛" (3 mm) instead of the traditional ¼" (6 mm). You need to clip the curve of a "U," the inside curve of the tulip, the valley of a "V," and any other place where the needle seems to drag.

Q. Must I stitch through all the fabric layers?

A. It's not necessary.

Q. What if a dark design piece placed under a light design piece shows through?

A. Let it wear a slip as you would under a sheer dress. Cut a piece of voile, organza, or organdy the same shape as your template (do not add seam allowance) and sandwich it between the dark and the light.

Q. What if a point frays?

A. Don't let it distress you. Consider the fray your seam allowance and turn those threads under with your needle.

Q. What if I clip the "V" too deep?

A. Don't worry. Just make it a little deeper at that point.

Q. What if a thread of the DF "eeks" out?

A. Push it back in with your needle.

Q. Must the stitches on the back all go in the same direction?

A. . Don't worry about the back stitches. Focus on the front ones.

Q. What if the circle doesn't come out at the same place I began?

A. Snip the knot and take out two or more stitches.

Reshape the circle and finish stitching.

Q. Do I appliqué bias stems on both sides?

A. Yes.

Q. Do I press seams open or to one side?

A. You decide, but, when assembling the top, pressing them open makes quilting easier.

Q. Do I iron the bias?

A. Iron the fabric before cutting, but not afterwards because pressing can stretch bias.

Q. Do I cut away the background fabric from behind the design after I finish appliquéing?

A. You decide, but the batt will sink in the cut out places.

Q. What quilting design should I use?

A. A simple one that will not compete with the Jacobean design.

Q. Do I quilt on the design fabric pieces?

A. No, shadow quilt and echo quilt two or three times out from the design.

Q. Will dry cleaning take out pencil marks?

A. No, not usually. Ask your cleaner.

Q. What is the best way to store quilts?

A. Ideally out flat on a bed, piled high like in "The Princess and the Pea," and covered to deter animals and sunshine.

Q. What are the best brands to use?

A. These products were used in making the featured quilt ROMANTICA. Neither Pat nor Mimi is affiliated with any of the named companies.

Fabric
  Gutcheon's "American Classic"™
  RJR
  Alexander Henry
  Hoffman
  Skydyes
  P & B

Thread
  Mettler #60 machine embroidery
  DMC #50 machine embroidery
  Gutermann quilting

Scissors
  Fiskar® 5" sharp point
  Gingher® 4" embroidery

Needles
  Clover #12 Betweens

Quilting Pins
  Dritz®

Pencils
  Berol Prismacolor®

Pens
  Sharpie®
  Pigma

Batting
  Hobbs

Quilt Frame
  Morgan Craft Stand
  The Flynn Quilt Frame

THE STUDENTS

These photographs are of the quilts made by participants in the workshop conducted to test patterns for ROMANTICA. Isn't it incredible that seven people could all use the same pattern and present such different creations? Aren't you encouraged to try your wings and see where they will take you?

Top: SHARON CHAMBERS, MESQUITE, TEXAS. Quilter, homemaker, grandmother, interviewer. "After many years of quiltmaking I discovered Jacobean appliqué. The flow of the patterns made appliqué easy and makes me look like a pro."

Bottom left: JOAN WEBB COWDREY, DALLAS, TEXAS. Retired, late blooming quilter. "Color selection seemed a problem initially, but this project urged me to follow my own drummer to add confidence."

Bottom right: BETTY DAY COX, DALLAS, TEXAS. Former biology teacher, volunteer, stitcher, reader, native Mississippian. "Having done little appliqué in the past, this was a real challenge. The experience has given me a better eye for color, a better understanding of appliqué techniques, and a quilt to be proud of."

Page 157
Top left: SONDRA COOL GORDON, PLANO, TEXAS. Grandmother, volunteer, seamstress, Christian, wife, and mother. "As a person who loves soft colors and pastels, this quilt was a real challenge. It was extremely

interesting to see how the bright colors combined to produce a pleasing effect."

Bottom left, : ROXANNE CHOATE RENTZEL,
VAN ALYSTYNE, TEXAS.
Quilter, quilt shop owner, teacher. *"This class set me free to do appliqué. I had always struggled with it until making this quilt. It was a challenge, a great learning experience, and most rewarding when the blocks were completed."*

Top right: J. COLLEEN FRY SEGROVES, PLANO, TEXAS.
Fabric artist, retired United Methodist clergy, wife, mom, grand-

mother. *"As a nontraditional quilter, I like paint with fabric in a realistic manner. Appliqué is a favorite technique because it keeps me awake while watching TV, is portable, and generally doesn't repeat the same thing a zillion times."*
Machine quilting by Schley Sisson.

Bottom right: RITA GALE RUSZXZYK, DALLAS TEXAS.
Graduate of the Traphagen School of Fashion, New York City. *"A quilter's work is a reflection of her spirit! Quiltmaking is an excellent way to express one's most sincere feelings."*

THE STITCHERS

Block 1
RUTH KOCK
PORT ELIZABETH, SOUTH AFRICA
An exceptionally busy estate agent who wishes she had more time for her hobby of quiltmaking.
"I was elated to receive this block to do. But I know it's not my 'expertise' that was wanted, but friendship – which cannot be ensured any other way."

Block 2
ARLETHA L. RAYMOND
FREMONT, CALIFORNIA
Housewife, mother, and grandmother, who is also a dreamer – dreaming of the next project.
"I have been doing serious appliqué – my favorite form of needleart – since 1992. This is my first attempt at Jacobean appliqué and I have fallen in love with it."

Block 3
JO QUIRAM
PLAINVIEW, MINNESOTA
Wife, mother, avid reader, energetic volunteer.
"Pat Campbell is a talented artist. Her appliqué technique is excellent. If you ever have an opportunity to take a class from her, do it."

Block 4
JAN SCHULZ
AUSTIN, MINNESOTA
Nurse, mother, grandmother, quilt show junkie.
"It was an honor to be asked to do this block. I enjoyed it very much."

Block 5
SALLY BARNES
MANHATTAN BEACH, CALIFORNIA
Quilter, wife, quilt shop clerk and teacher, reader, and mini-dachshund owner.
"I love quilting in bright colors and Jacobean appliqué is a natural."

Block 6
MARSHA S. DARDENNE
ST. FRANCISVILLE, LOUISIANA
Obsessive, compulsive, addictive, Anglophile, history, and antique lover.
"I enjoy intricate appliqué, because hand needlework is my favorite. I feel like the quote from an antique sampler: 'I pray that, risen from the dead, I may in Glory stand…. A crown, perhaps, upon my head, But a needle in my hand!'"

Block 7
CYNDEE BROWN
BATON ROUGE, LOUISIANA
Mom, wife, craft enthusiast.
"I had not done any appliqué for several months and doing this block got my creative juices going again. I'm ready to start a new project immediately."

Block 8
MAE MARRS LUIGS
GARLAND, TEXAS
Quilter, mother, grandmother, teacher.
"I'd only done traditional appliqué before, so using the wild prints and colors of these fabrics has been an enlightening experience that has broadened my range of materials."

Block 9 and Top Border
PAM GOLDKORN
DURBAN, SOUTH AFRICA
Wife, mother, reverse appliquér.
"I found this appliqué challenging. I was nervous because the fabric had come from America (so far away) and I had no 'back-up' fabric to help me out of a 'jam' if the need arose (which it didn't)."

Block 10
SHIONA CLARK
PORT ELIZABETH, SOUTH AFRICA
Mother, Scot, dreamer, optimist, pessimist.
"I'm the accidental quilter. I didn't even know other people still made quilts when I made my first one – on the machine. And by machine I still do it, so how did I get persuaded to stitch an appliqué block by hand? Flattery will get you anywhere! "

Block 11
KATHY JARDINE
DUBLIN, CALIFORNIA
Anglophile, family historian, traveler, gardener, bibliophile.
"I was not bored for one second while making this block. The unique designs and use of color create great visual excitement. I can hardly wait to see the entire quilt."

Block 12
BERYL HEALY
PORT ELIZABETH, SOUTH AFRICA
Mother, lover of scuba diving, camping, and outdoors, new quilter.
"Being a machine quilter, I never knew how enjoyable handwork could be until I did this block."

Right Border
TERRY MONSON
ROSCOE, ILLINOIS
Mother, fabric connoisseur, health food gourmet.
"I enjoyed working on Romantica, especially the bright colors."

Left Border
STEPHANIA L. BOMMARITO
TORRANCE, CALIFORNIA
Quilter, lover of gardens, children , and life.
"Just as my mother always spent time growing beautiful flowers in her garden, I enjoy quilting flowers of many kinds. Being able to help a friend grow an exquisitely planned garden with beautiful colors and patterns was a special joy."

Bottom Border
INA ERICSON
RICHARDSON, TEXAS
Wife, mother, quilter, machine sewer, fisherwoman, RV camper, patriotic American, photographer, and lover of life.
"My mother instilled in me the love of sewing at the very early age of five. I've done many creative things in my life including lapidary, porcelain doll making, and ceramics, but I always come back to sewing."

Corner Blocks
SHARON CHAMBERS
MESQUITE, TEXAS
Quilter, interviewer, homemaker.

"Quilting has been my salvation during a mid-life crisis. The Jacobean appliqué flows so nicely. The pieces look difficult but are easy to do."

Drafting
MICHELLE JACK
GARLAND, TEXAS

Quilting
THEKLA SCHNITKER
HOYLETON, ILLINOIS

Figures
MIMI AYARS
BEDFORD, TEXAS

1995 AQS Quilt Contest!!!

Entry Blank To Accompany Slides (may be photocopied)

Membership #_____

Name(s) _____
    (Please Print)   **List additional names on back of entry form.**

Street _____

City_____ State ____ Zip _____

Phone (_____)_____

Local Newspaper_____

Circle **One** Category Number:

1. Applique, Ama.	8. Group, Ama. or Pro.
2. Applique, Pro.	9. Miniature, Ama. or Pro.
3. Trad. Pieced, Ama.	10. Wall, Ama.
4. Trad. Pieced, Pro.	11. Wall, Pro.
5. Innov. Pieced, Ama.	12. Pict. Wall, Ama. or Pro.
6. Innov. Pieced, Pro.	13. Theme Wall, Ama. or Pro.
7. Other Tech., Ama or Pro.	

Original Design: ☐ Yes   ☐ No
Quilted by: ☐ Hand   ☐ Machine

Quilt Title _____

Quilt Size (inches) _____" w x _____"l _____

Basic Techniques _____

Brief Description of Quilt for Show Booklet _____
_____

Approximate Insurance Value $_____
           (Maximum $5,000.00)

I wish to enter the above item and agree to abide by the quilt contest rules & decisions of the jury and judges. I understand that AQS will take every precaution to protect my quilt exhibited in this show. I realize they cannot be responsible for the acts of nature beyond their control. You may have my permission to photograph this quilt. If my quilt is exhibited in the American Quilter's Society Show, I understand that my signature gives AQS the right to use a photo of my quilt in any publications, advertisements, or promotional materials.

Signature _____

Social Security # _____
Please put your name on the slide mounts & mail slides, entry blank & 58¢ SASE to: **American Quilter's Society,** Klaudeen Hansen, P.O. Box 3290, Dept. Entry, Paducah, KY 42002-3290.

≈ American Quilter's Society ≈
dedicated to publishing books for today's quilters

The following AQS publications are currently available:

- **Adapting Architectural Details for Quilts,** Carol Wagner, #2282: AQS, 1992, 88 pages, softbound, $12.95
- **American Beauties: Rose & Tulip Quilts,** Gwen Marston & Joe Cunningham, #1907: AQS, 1988, 96 pages, softbound, $14.95
- **Appliqué Designs: My Mother Taught Me to Sew,** Faye Anderson, #2121: AQS, 1990, 80 pages, softbound, $12.95
- **Appliqué Patterns from Native American Beadwork Designs,** Dr. Joyce Mori, #3790: AQS, 1994, 96 pages, softbound, $14.95
- **The Art of Hand Appliqué,** Laura Lee Fritz, #2122: AQS, 1990, 80 pages, softbound, $14.95
- **...Ask Helen More About Quilting Designs,** Helen Squire, #2099: AQS, 1990, 54 pages, 17 x 11, spiral-bound, $14.95
- **Award-Winning Quilts & Their Makers, Vol. I: The Best of AQS Shows – 1985-1987,** #2207: AQS, 1991, 232 pages, softbound, $24.95
- **Award-Winning Quilts & Their Makers, Vol. II: The Best of AQS Shows – 1988-1989,** #2354: AQS, 1992, 176 pages, softbound, $24.95
- **Award-Winning Quilts & Their Makers, Vol. III: The Best of AQS Shows – 1990-1991,** #3425: AQS, 1993, 180 pages, softbound, $24.95
- **Award-Winning Quilts & Their Makers, Vol. IV: The Best of AQS Shows – 1992-1993,** #3791: AQS, 1994, 180 pages, softbound, $24.95
- **Celtic Style Floral Appliqué: Designs Using Interlaced Scrollwork,** Scarlett Rose, #3926: AQS, 1995, 128 pages, softbound, $14.95
- **Classic Basket Quilts,** Elizabeth Porter & Marianne Fons, #2208: AQS, 1991, 128 pages, softbound, $16.95
- **A Collection of Favorite Quilts,** Judy Florence, #2119: AQS, 1990, 136 pages, softbound, $18.95
- **Creative Machine Art,** Sharee Dawn Roberts, #2355: AQS, 1992, 142 pages, 9 x 9, softbound, $24.95
- **Dear Helen, Can You Tell Me?...All About Quilting Designs,** Helen Squire, #1820: AQS, 1987, 51 pages, 17 x 11, spiral-bound, $12.95
- **Double Wedding Ring Quilts: New Quilts from an Old Favorite,** #3870: AQS, 1994, 112 pages, softbound, $14.95
- **Dye Painting!,** Ann Johnston, #3399: AQS, 1992, 88 pages, softbound, $19.95
- **Dyeing & Overdyeing of Cotton Fabrics,** Judy Mercer Tescher, #2030: AQS, 1990, 54 pages, softbound, $9.95
- **Encyclopedia of Pieced Quilt Patterns,** compiled by Barbara Brackman, #3468: AQS, 1993, 552 pages, hardbound, $34.95
- **Fabric Postcards: Landmarks & Landscapes • Monuments & Meadows,** Judi Warren, #3846: AQS, 1994, 120 pages, softbound, $22.95
- **Flavor Quilts for Kids to Make: Complete Instructions for Teaching Children to Dye, Decorate & Sew Quilts,** Jennifer Amor, #2356. AQS, 1991, 120 pages, softbound, $12.95
- **From Basics to Binding: A Complete Guide to Making Quilts,** Karen Kay Buckley, #2381: AQS, 1992, 160 pages, softbound, $16.95
- **Fun & Fancy Machine Quiltmaking,** Lois Smith, #1982: AQS, 1989, 144 pages, softbound, $19.95
- **Gatherings: America's Quilt Heritge** Kathlyn F. Sullivan, #4526: AQS, 1995, 224 pages, 10 x 8½, softbound, $34.95
- **Heirloom Miniatures,** Tina M. Gravatt, #2097: AQS, 1990, 64 pages, softbound, $9.95
- **Infinite Stars,** Gayle Bong, #2283: AQS, 1992, 72 pages, softbound, $12.95
- **The Ins and Outs: Perfecting the Quilting Stitch,** Patricia J. Morris, #2120: AQS, 1990, 96 pages, softbound, $9.95
- **Irish Chain Quilts: A Workbook of Irish Chains & Related Patterns,** Joyce B. Peaden, #1906: AQS, 1988, 96 pages, softbound, $14.95
- **Jacobean Appliqué: Book I, "Exotica,"** Patricia B. Campbell & Mimi Ayars, Ph.D, #3784: AQS, 1993, 160 pages, softbound, $18.95
- **Jacobean Appliqué: Book II, "Romantica,"** Patricia B. Campbell & Mimi Ayars, Ph.D, #4544: AQS, 1995, 160 pages, softbound, $18.95
- **The Judge's Task: How Award-Winning Quilts Are Selected,** Patricia J. Morris, #3904: AQS, 1993, 128 pages, softbound, $19.95
- **Log Cabin Quilts: New Quilts from an Old Favorite,** edited by Victoria Faoro, #4523: AQS, 1995, 128 pages, softbound, $14.95
- **Marbling Fabrics for Quilts: A Guide for Learning & Teaching,** Kathy Fawcett & Carol Shoaf, #2206: AQS, 1991, 72 pages, softbound, $12.95
- **Mola Techniques for Today's Quilters,** Charlotte Patera, #4514: AQS, 1995, 112 pages, softbound, $18.95
- **More Projects and Patterns: A Second Collection of Favorite Quilts,** Judy Florence, #3330: AQS, 1992, 152 pages, softbound, $18.95
- **Nancy Crow: Quilts and Influences,** Nancy Crow, #1981: AQS, 1990, 256 pages, 9 x 12, hardcover, $29.95
- **Nancy Crow: Work in Transition,** Nancy Crow, #3331: AQS, 1992, 32 pages, 9 x 10, softbound, $12.95
- **New Jersey Quilts – 1777 to 1950: Contributions to an American Tradition,** The Heritage Quilt Project of New Jersey; text by Rachel Cochran, Rita Erickson, Natalie Hart & Barbara Schaffer, #3332: AQS, 1992, 256 pages, softbound, $29.95
- **New Patterns from Old Architecture,** Carol Wagner, #3927: AQS, 1995, 72 pages, softbound, $12.95
- **No Dragons on My Quilt,** Jean Ray Laury with Ritva Laury & Lizabeth Laury, #2153: AQS, 1990, 52 pages, hardcover, $12.95
- **Old Favorites in Miniature,** Tina Gravatt, #3469: AQS, 1993, 104 pages, softbound, $15.95
- **A Patchwork of Pieces: An Anthology of Early Quilt Stories 1845-1940,** complied by Cuesta Ray Benberry and Carol Pinney Crabb, #3333: AQS, 1993, 360 pages, 5½ x 8½, softbound, $14.95
- **Precision Patchwork for Scrap Quilts, Anytime, Anywhere…,** Jeannette Muir, #3928: AQS, 1995, 72 pages, softbound, $12.95
- **Quilt Groups Today: Who They Are, Where They Meet, What They Do, and How to Contact Them – A Complete Guide for 1992-1993,** #3308: AQS, 1992, 336 pages, softbound, $14.95
- **Quilter's Registry,** Lynne Fritz, #2380: AQS, 1992, 80 pages, 5½ x 8½, hardbound, $9.95
- **Quilting Patterns from Native American Designs,** Dr. Joyce Mori, #3467: AQS, 1993, 80 pages, softbound, $12.95
- **Quilting With Style: Principles for Great Pattern Design,** Gwen Marston & Joe Cunningham, #3470: AQS, 1993, 192 pages, hardbound, $24.95
- **Quiltmaker's Guide: Basics & Beyond,** Carol Doak, #2284: AQS, 1992, 208 pages, softbound, $19.95
- **Quilts: The Permanent Collection –** MAQS, #2257: AQS, 1991, 100 pages, 10 x 6½, softbound, $9.95
- **Quilts: The Permanent Collection – MAQS, Volume II,** #3793: AQS, 1994, 80 pages, 10 x 6½, softbound, $9.95
- **Roots, Feathers & Blooms: 4-Block Quilts, Their History & Patterns, Book I,** Linda Giesler Carlson, #3789: AQS, 1994, 128 pages, softbound, $16.95
- **Seasons of the Heart & Home: Quilts for a Winter's Day,** Jan Patek, #3796: AQS, 1993, 160 pages, softbound, $18.95
- **Seasons of the Heart & Home: Quilts for Summer Days,** Jan Patek, #3761: AQS, 1993, 160 pages, softbound, $18.95
- **Sensational Scrap Quilts,** Darra Duffy Williamson, #2357: AQS, 1992, 152 pages, softbound, $24.95
- **Show Me Helen...How to Use Quilting Designs,** Helen Squire, #3375: AQS, 1993, 155 pages, softbound, $15.95
- **Somewhere in Between: Quilts and Quilters of Illinois,** Rita Barrow Barber, #1790: AQS, 1986, 78 pages, softbound, $14.95
- **Spike & Zola: Patterns for Laughter…and Appliqué, Painting, or Stenciling,** Donna French Collins, #3794: AQS, 1993, 72 pages, softbound, $9.95
- **The Stori Book of Embellishing: Great Ideas for Quilts and Garments,** Mary Stori, #3929: AQS, 1994, 96 pages, softbound, $16.95
- **Straight Stitch Machine Appliqué: History, Patterns & Instructions for This Easy Technique,** Letty Martin, #3903: AQS, 1994, 160 pages, softbound, $16.95
- **Striplate Piecing: Piecing Circle Designs with Speed and Accuracy,** Debra Wagner, #3792: AQS, 1994, 168 pages 9 x 12, hardbound, $24.95
- **Tessellations and Variations: Creating One-Patch & Two-Patch Quilts,** Barbara Ann Caron, #3930: AQS, 1994, 120 pages, softbound, $14.95
- **Three-Dimensional Appliqué and Embroidery Embellishment: Techniques for Today's Album Quilt,** Anita Shackelford, #3788: AQS, 1993, 152 pages, 9 x 12, hardbound, $24.95
- **Time-Span Quilts: New Quilts from Old Tops,** Becky Herdle, #3931: AQS, 1994, 136 pages, softbound, $16.95
- **A Treasury of Quilting Designs,** Linda Goodmon Emery, #2029: AQS, 1990, 80 pages, 14 x 11, spiral-bound, $14.95
- **Tricks with Chintz: Using Large Prints to Add New Magic to Traditional Quilt Blocks,** Nancy S. Breland, #3847: AQS, 1994, 96 pages, softbound, $14.95
- **Wonderful Wearables: A Celebration of Creative Clothing,** Virginia Avery, #2286: AQS, 1991, 184 pages, softbound, $24.95

These books can be found in local bookstores and quilt shops. If you are unable to locate a title in your area, you can order by mail from AQS, P.O. Box 3290, Paducah, KY 42002-3290. Please add $2 for the first book and 40¢ for each additional one to cover postage and handling. (International orders please add $2.50 for the first book and $1 for each additional one.)